A WORLD BANK STUDY

Suspending Suspicious Transactions

Klaudijo Stroligo, Horst Intscher, and Susan Davis-Crockwell

THE WORLD BANK
Washington, D.C.

Contents

Boxes

Tables

Acknowledgments

This report is based on the World Bank–Egmont Group study on Financial Intelligence Unit (FIU) power to postpone suspicious transactions, and is a joint effort of the project team composed of members of the Financial Market Integrity Unit, Financial and Private Sector Development (FFSFI), of the World Bank, and the Egmont Legal Working Group. It was written by Klaudijo Stroligo (Senior Financial Sector Specialist and Team Leader, World Bank), Horst Intscher (Consultant, World Bank, and former Head of FIU Canada), and Susan Davis-Crockwell (Senior Legal Counsel, FIU Bermuda), under the direction of Jean Pesme (Manager, World Bank).

The team benefited significantly from oral and written comments received during the peer review process and wishes to thank the following peer reviewers who helped finalize the concept note and/or shape this report: Satyadev Deonarain Bikoo (Director of FIU Mauritius), Paolo Costanzo (Chairman of the Egmont Legal Working Group, FIU Italy), Giuseppe Lombardo (Senior Counsel, Legal Department, International Monetary Fund), Marianne Mathias (Consultant, FFSFI, World Bank), Richard Nash (Counsel, Justice Reform Practice Group, World Bank), Ric Power (AML Adviser/Law Enforcement, United Nations Office on Drugs and Crime–Global Programme against Money-Laundering), and Boudewijn Verhelst (Egmont Group Chairmen and Deputy Head of FIU Belgium).

The team is also grateful to members of the Egmont Legal Working Group for their willingness to read multiple drafts of this report and their constant support of the project. In particular, the team wishes to thank Katerina Buhayets, Shoba Kammula, and Olivier Lenert for their useful comments.

Most important, the team would like to acknowledge the important contributions made by the FIUs that participated in the World Bank–Egmont Group 2011 survey and those that contributed supplementary information about their practical experiences in the use of the power to postpone suspicious transactions.

Klaudijo Stroligo
Task Team Leader
Financial Market Integrity Unit
World Bank

About the Authors

Susan Davis-Crockwell is the Senior Legal Counsel with the Financial Intelligence Agency (the "FIA") in Bermuda and assisted with its formation in November 2008. Ms. Davis-Crockwell is responsible for advising the FIA on the legality of all issues arising within and affecting the FIA. Ms. Davis-Crockwell has been an active member of the Egmont Group since 2009 and is currently the Vice Chair of the Legal Working Group.

Prior to joining the FIA, Ms. Davis-Crockwell spent four years working within the Government of Bermuda, first as the Assistant Official Receiver of Bermuda and then as a Senior Crown Counsel within the Ministry of Justice. In both of these capacities, she has held a seat on Bermuda's National Anti-Money Laundering Committee, which is the Intra-Governmental Committee responsible for advising the Minister of Justice on matters relating to the detection and prevention of money laundering and terrorist financing.

Ms. Davis-Crockwell began her legal career in private practice working at the law firm of Appleby for seven years. She holds an LLB (Hons) and has been called to Bars of England & Wales and Bermuda.

Horst Intscher founded the Canadian financial intelligence unit (FINTRAC) and served as Director and CEO of that independent federal agency from 2000 to 2008. Since 2008, he has worked as an AML/CFT consultant for the World Bank and the IMF. He was a team member of a 2008–09 joint WB/Egmont Group study of governance arrangements of FIUs. He also participated in four Mutual Evaluations. During his tenure as Director of FINTRAC, Mr. Intscher was actively involved in the Egmont Group, as Vice Chair of the Egmont Committee, Chair of the Egmont Transition Sub-Committee, and Chair of the IT Working Group. Prior to establishing FINTRAC, Mr. Intscher had an extensive career in the Canadian public service as a senior policy executive in the areas of law enforcement, intelligence, and national security, as Assistant Secretary to Cabinet (Security and Intelligence), and later as Assistant Deputy Solicitor General (Policy). In the latter role, he was responsible for the development of several initiatives for combatting organized crime, including the initiative that led to the establishment of the Canadian FIU.

Klaudijo Stroligo is the Senior Financial Sector Specialist in the Financial and Private Sector Development Unit of the World Bank and until April 2012 he was also the joint World Bank/UNODC anti-money laundering and countering terrorist financing Mentor for Central Asia. In 2006–07, he was a consultant for the World Bank, Council of Europe, European Commission, IMF, and UNODC.

Previously he was the Director of the Slovenian Financial Intelligence Unit and served in this capacity for 12 years. Earlier in his career, Mr Stroligo was a Crime Inspector and Head of Foreign Crime Department in the Crime Police Unit in Ljubljana and in the Ministry of Interior of Slovenia.

For several years, he was the Chairman and Vice-Chairman of the Council of Europe Moneyval Committee and member of four other expert committees of Council of Europe responsible for drafting conventions and recommendations related to seizure and confiscation of proceeds of crime, economic and organized crime, money laundering, terrorist financing, and corruption. Mr. Stroligo was actively involved in the Egmont Group, as one of the funding members and as a member of the Egmont Group Committee and Legal Working Group.

Acronyms and Abbreviations

AML/CFT	anti-money laundering/countering financing of terrorism
CTIF-CFI	Belgian Financial Intelligence Processing Unit
CTR	Currency Transaction Report
DNFBPs	Designated Non-Financial Businesses and Professions
EU	European Union
FATF	Financial Action Task Force
FIUs	Financial Intelligence Units
FSRBs	FATF-Style Regional Bodies
IMF	International Monetary Fund
LEA	law enforcement authority
ML/FT	money laundering/financing of terrorism
STR	Suspicious Transaction Report

Strasbourg Convention   Council of Europe Convention on Laundering, Search, Seizure, and Confiscation of the Proceeds from Crime

Third EU AML/CFT Directive   European Union Directive 2005/60/EC on the Prevention of the Use of the Financial System for the Purpose of Money Laundering and Terrorist Financing

UN	United Nations
UNCAC	United Nations Convention against Corruption
UNODC	United Nations Office on Drugs and Crime
UNSC	United Nations Security Council
UNTOC	United Nations Convention against Transnational Organized Crime, or the Palermo Convention
VAT	value-added tax

Warsaw Convention   Council of Europe Convention on Laundering, Search, Seizure, and Confiscation of the Proceeds from Crime and on the Financing of Terrorism

Executive Summary

Financial Intelligence Units

Financial Intelligence Units (FIUs) are national bodies created to receive reports of suspicious transactions from financial institutions and other designated reporting entities, to analyze and elaborate those reports with additional information from a wide range of other sources, and to disseminate financial intelligence reports about suspected money laundering or terrorism financing to appropriate law enforcement agencies in their country. When appropriate, FIUs may also share such information with counterpart organizations in other jurisdictions.

The Power to Postpone Suspicious Transactions

One of the powers held by many, but not all, FIUs is the administrative power to order the postponement of reported suspicious transactions as a means of preventing the flight of suspect funds or assets beyond the reach of national law enforcement and prosecutorial authorities during the time it takes for those national authorities to seek and obtain a freezing or seizing order from the judicial or other competent authorities. Although a significant number of FIUs have possessed this power for some time, there is very little documented information about the nature and extent of the legal basis and arrangements for such powers, about the measures available to exercise these powers, and operational issues that arise in the exercise of these powers.

A Joint World Bank–Egmont Group Study of the Power to Postpone

The Egmont Group is an international association of 131 FIUs.[1] It represents and supports member FIUs, and undertakes a variety of initiatives to strengthen the capacity of member FIUs to fulfill their mandates within the larger national and international initiatives to combat money laundering and terrorism financing. Similarly, an important element of the World Bank's programming focuses on measures to strengthen the capacity of member countries to combat money laundering, terrorism financing, and corruption, and to assist countries in locating, tracking, and recovering stolen assets. In light of these shared interests, the World Bank and the Egmont Group undertook a joint study of the FIU power to postpone suspicious transactions, to gather and publish information about arrangements authorizing FIUs to postpone transactions, and about the operational practices and experiences found in the use of this power.

A joint World Bank–Egmont Group project team was established to develop and administer a comprehensive survey that in May 2011 was sent to 134 FIUs (120 Egmont members and 14 others), which yielded responses from 88 FIUs. The survey consisted of 58 questions covering a wide range of topics and issues, including the legal basis of the postponement power, conditions or restrictions on its application, the scope of application, factors influencing the discretionary application, maximum duration of postponement orders, informing the subject or suspect, right of appeal, and postponements on behalf of foreign FIUs. The survey also sought information on a variety of operational issues, including timeliness of access to necessary information, capacity to respond, operational procedures, steps and factors considered in making a postponement decision, and follow-up to postponement orders. The survey also sought statistical information on a range of factors related to the frequency of the use of the postponement power, and results flowing from postponements of suspicious transactions.

Sixty-two (70 percent) of the respondent FIUs indicated that they have the power to postpone transactions. In addition, the survey provided a number of interesting, sometimes surprising, findings.

Most of the FIUs making postponements have an explicit legal basis for their action, but a small number of FIUs apply this power without apparent statutory authority. There is significant variation in the scope of the application of the power, and there is a variety of conditions or influencing factors in application, and a range of factors or conditions that can trigger use of the power. The reported duration of postponement orders ranges from one day to six months, or longer. Only half of the postponements fall in the range of two to five days. Almost half of the participating FIUs have the authority to issue oral postponements in urgent cases. In only nine jurisdictions is it required that the client be informed of a postponement order. In 35 jurisdictions, laws do not provide for a right of appeal of a postponement order. Thirty-nine FIUs can issue a postponement order on behalf of a foreign FIU, and the same number (though not necessarily the same FIUs) can request a foreign FIU to make a postponement.

The survey data show that while 62 FIUs have the power to postpone, about 27 percent did not use the power at all in the three-year period covered by the survey, and 16 percent used it only infrequently (one to three times) during the period. In 2010, 54 FIUs reported issuing an aggregate total of 1,412 postponement orders. A mere 6 FIUs accounted for 62 percent of those postponements.

Recommendations

Based on the findings of the survey, a number of issues have been highlighted in respect of which FIUs may wish to consider possible improvements or restraints in the way in which the postponement power is used. This report contains 16 recommendations intended to provide perspective and guidance on sound practice. **The recommendations are not intended to advocate the use of the postponement power, nor the acquisition of it by FIUs that do not already have it. Rather, they are intended to provide advice and explanation to those FIUs that already use the power, and "how to" advice to others that may wish to acquire this power.**

A guiding principle of these recommendations is that they endeavor to strengthen the rule of law and enhance the transparency of postponement of transactions and ensuing seizures and confiscations.

Briefly summarized, these recommendations are as follows:

- Provide an explicit legal basis for the FIU's power to postpone suspicious transactions.
- Ensure that the postponement decision remains with the FIU.
- Identify the minimum requisite conditions for the FIU's exercise of this power.
- Apply the postponement power to transactions related to suspected money laundering, associated predicate offenses, and suspected terrorism financing.
- Apply the postponement power to transactions conducted at financial institutions, and at Designated Non-Financial Businesses and Professions, if the nature of the transaction permits such an action to be taken.
- Ensure that legislation mandates a reasonable maximum duration for the FIU postponement order.
- The law should allow the FIU to cancel a postponement order before its expiry if the reasons for postponement cease to exist.
- Ensure that reporting entities, FIUs, and their representatives are protected by law from criminal and civil liability for damages caused by a postponement order if it was carried out lawfully and in good faith.
- Avoid using the FIU power to postpone transactions in the freezing process under United Nations Security Council Resolutions related to terrorism if there is no regulated complementary freezing procedure carried out by another competent authority.
- Introduce legal provisions to require the FIU to issue a written postponement order, while allowing for an oral order in urgent cases when the nature of the transaction does not allow sufficient time to issue a written order.
- Consider adopting legislative measures to permit the FIU to request a foreign FIU to postpone a transaction on its behalf, and to postpone a transaction at the request of a foreign FIU.
- Promote and facilitate the effective use by FIUs of their power to postpone suspicious transactions.

- Develop and implement training of FIU and reporting entity staff on the procedures for use and application of the postponement power.
- Develop and implement collection by the FIU of comprehensive operational statistics on the use of the power to postpone transactions and the follow-on actions that flow from those postponements.
- Develop and implement effective mechanisms for coordination of the activities of reporting entities and public authorities involved in the postponement of transactions and follow-on interventions that may be triggered by the postponement.

Note

1. As of July 2012.

CHAPTER 1

Introduction

Serious economic crime, grand corruption, and organized crime are by their nature international and also extremely profitable. According to the 2010 United Nations Office on Drugs and Crime (UNODC) publication, "The Globalization of Crime," organized crime is one of the world's most sophisticated and profitable businesses; it has diversified, gone global, and reached macroeconomic proportions.[1] Consequently, the effective fight against such crimes requires the use of modern and effective methods at both the domestic and international levels. Over the last two decades, the domestic and international law enforcement strategies have increasingly focused on the financial aspects of these forms of crime, thus targeting the economic power of criminals. These strategies aim at both identifying and prosecuting the higher-level criminals and their gatekeepers, who are usually not involved in committing the initial criminal offenses, and at preventing them from benefiting from, or making use of, the proceeds of crime.

To that end, several international and regional conventions have been adopted that require jurisdictions to adopt legislative and other measures to enable them to confiscate proceeds of crime and instrumentalities, or property the value of which corresponds to such proceeds and laundered property.[2] International standards also require jurisdictions to establish mechanisms to rapidly identify, trace, freeze, or seize any property that is liable to confiscation. Furthermore, according to these standards, jurisdictions are required to develop effective strategies for anti-money laundering and countering financing of terrorism (AML/CFT) and establish a related legal and institutional framework.

As an important element of these strategies, financial intelligence units (FIUs) began to be created in the early 1990s as national centers for receiving, requesting, analyzing, and disseminating suspicious transaction reports (STRs) and other information regarding potential money laundering and terrorist financing. Since then, FIUs have been established in more than 150 jurisdictions and, as of July 2012, FIUs from 131 jurisdictions have been admitted to the Egmont Group.[3]

In addition to the core functions, many FIUs are also mandated to perform other functions, such as (a) drafting AML/CFT legislation, (b) monitoring compliance of reporting entities, (c) training of reporting entities, and (d) postponing suspicious transactions.[4] While the FIU core functions are regulated and evaluated internationally throughout the Egmont Group membership process and Financial Action Task Force (FATF)/FATF-Style Regional Bodies (FSRBs)/International Monetary Fund (IMF)/World Bank[5] mutual assessment of overall AML/CFT frameworks, the FIU's additional functions are not treated in the same manner.

According to World Bank and Egmont Group data, the FIUs in at least 79 jurisdictions are authorized to postpone suspicious transactions related to money laundering, associated predicate offenses, terrorist financing, and/or other criminal offenses.[6] Jurisdictions developed this power mostly in response to the following practical problem.

In most jurisdictions the power to freeze or seize a transaction and/or money on deposit in bank accounts was given to judicial or prosecutorial and/or law enforcement authorities. These provisional measures are subject to establishing a level of suspicion, and other conditions that usually apply in criminal and precriminal procedures. Therefore, in practice, some judicial and/or law enforcement authorities have found it challenging to take urgent actions to prevent the completion of such transactions. By empowering FIUs to postpone suspicious transactions, these authorities gain some time to determine whether or not the provisional measures should be taken to prevent the dissipation of the assets.

Despite the significant number of FIUs with the power to postpone suspicious transactions, relatively little information has been compiled to date about the legal arrangements that have been developed to empower FIUs in this area, or about the circumstances, conditions, and challenges of the exercise of this power or the extent and frequency of its use.[7] Moreover, there are no universal international standards regulating the FIU power to postpone suspicious transactions, and only at the European level does an international legal instrument dealing explicitly with this topic exist.[8]

In response to a growing demand for reliable information about the legal and operational arrangements, and about practices and challenges relevant to the use of this FIU power, the World Bank and the Egmont Group decided in March 2011 to carry out a joint study of FIUs to gather more information in this regard. The main objectives of this study are to:

• Inform the policy discussion on the postponement power
• Provide guidance to FIUs that already have, or are considering, acquiring the power to postpone suspicious transactions with a view to improving their existing postponement regimes or shaping new ones.

This joint study was intended to capture the widest possible cross section of FIUs.[9] However, the highest number of respondents were from European countries.[10] While the study had no control over the response rate, the respondent FIUs are nonetheless representative of the overall population of FIUs on dimensions such as type and size of FIU and geographic representation, and provide valuable information relevant for all FIUs with postponement power.

This report presents the results of the above-mentioned study, which, among other things, shows the existence of a wide range of practices and arrangements, and some gaps or omissions, in respect of a number of important aspects of the FIU power to postpone suspicious transactions. The study also indicates that only a relatively small proportion of FIUs with the power to postpone suspicious transactions are regular users of this power, while a substantial number have not used the power at all during the three-year period covered by the study, or have done so infrequently. The reasons for such performance by FIUs, and the answers to several complex issues, which were identified during the study, cannot be interpreted and explained reliably without gathering additional and more focused information, possibly through a follow-up study.

In addition, this report presents a number of recommendations to help FIU practitioners and policy makers establish or strengthen effective legal and operational mechanisms for the postponement of suspicious transactions, while taking into account the international FIU standards, and the rule of law, in order to ensure that the fundamental rights of all those concerned are effectively protected. The recommendations highlight issues and associated risks identified during the study and are meant, among other things, to facilitate the development of training and technical assistance initiatives in regard to the use of the FIU power to postpone suspicious transactions.

Finally, this report includes a number of sanitized cases provided by FIUs, and, where possible, examples of FIU legal and practical arrangements related to several recommendations. In addition, appendix D provides a template for a postponement order or notice, which FIUs may wish to use as guidance when drafting their own postponement orders.

Notes

1. United Nations Office on Drugs and Crime, "The Globalization of Crime— A Transnational Organized Crime Threat Assessment," Vienna, 2010, p. ii.

2. The United Nations Convention against Transnational Organized Crime (CTOC), known as the Palermo Convention (Article 12); the United Nations Convention against Corruption (UNCAC) (Article 31); the 1990 Council of Europe Convention on Laundering, Search, Seizure and Confiscation of the Proceeds from Crime, known as the Strasbourg Convention (Article 2); and the 2005 Council of Europe Convention on Laundering, Search, Seizure and Confiscation of the Proceeds from Crime and on the Financing of Terrorism, known as the Warsaw Convention (Articles 3 and 5).

3. The Egmont Group was established in 1995 as an informal international association of FIUs. Its goal is to provide a forum for FIUs around the world to improve cooperation in the fight against money laundering and financing of terrorism and to foster the implementation of domestic programs in this field. Egmont Group members are FIUs that comply with the criteria of the Egmont Group (http://www.egmontgroup .org). See also the "Egmont Group Annual Report 2010–2011," p. 24, http://www .egmontgroup.org/news-and-events/news/2011/12/23/2010-2011-egmont-group- annual-report).

4. IMF and World Bank, "Financial Intelligence Units–An Overview", Washington, DC, 2004, pp. 71–81.

5. The Financial Action Task Force/FATF-Style Regional Bodies/International Monetary Fund/World Bank.

6. This number is based on data provided in response to the Egmont 2010 Biennial Census and the World Bank–Egmont Group 2011 survey.

7. IMF and World Bank, "Financial Intelligence Units–An Overview," Washington, DC, 2004, pp. 75–79.

8. The Warsaw Convention.

9. See section "Overview of Responses" of appendix A.

10. This could possibly be attributed to the following facts: (a) the European region has a large number of small countries with a large concentration of financial centers compared to other regions, which, while accounting for a large percentage of the world's population, have fewer financial centers; and (b) FIUs have been in existence in this region longer than in other geographic regions, which may be in the process of developing or refining their FIUs. European FIUs, therefore, have more historical experience in administering the postponement power.

FIU Power to Postpone Suspicious Transactions–An Overview

The contemporary global fight against money laundering and financing of terrorism (ML/FT) is rooted in the fight against large-scale drug trafficking dating back to the 1970s. In addition to widespread social problems created by, or aggravated by, the significant and increasingly organized traffic in illicit drugs in North America and Europe, it soon came to the attention of authorities that the vast profits flowing from that growing illegal industry were giving rise to corrosive societal effects in the form of corruption and co-option. The legalization of proceeds was also undermining the integrity of financial institutions and intermediaries in a growing number of jurisdictions that were wittingly or unwittingly drawn into the ambit of illegal drug cartels.

Countries and international organizations responded to these challenges by greatly intensifying their fight against large-scale drug trafficking, and later on also against other forms of transnational economic and organized crime. It became even more obvious that the extremely lucrative profits of such crimes enriched perpetrators; corrupted or co-opted a range of businesses and professions; and facilitated the growth, organization, and diversification of criminal enterprise and the concealment or shielding of the profits and assets as well as perpetrators. This, in turn, led to the conviction that an intensified and global attack on transnational economic and organized crime was needed. International coordination was strengthened, international conventions were developed, and international organizations created programs to assist countries in strengthening their efforts to combat these criminal phenomena.

Anti-Money Laundering

By the 1980s, it became apparent that the campaign against drug trafficking needed to be accompanied by a similarly strong and systematic attack on illicit proceeds of serious criminal activity. Thus, by the mid-1980s, the anti-money-laundering campaign was born. Countries began to criminalize money laundering, and to develop legislated authorities and powers to facilitate the investigation and prosecution of money laundering and the confiscation of the proceeds of crime. Soon thereafter, the leaders of the most industrialized nations tasked their officials with developing recommendations for the implementation of comprehensive legislative, regulatory, investigative, and prosecutorial measures to address money laundering. The ensuing proposals were adopted during the G-7 Summit in France in July 1989. The Financial Action Task Force (FATF) was created to monitor the implementation of the measures, which became known as the FATF Recommendations.[1]

Since then, these recommendations have undergone several revisions and amplifications.[2] Moreover, in 2002, combating terrorism financing was added to what had by then become a global initiative to combat money laundering and terrorism financing.

Financial Intelligence Units

To facilitate the process of detecting assets and transactions that might derive from criminal activities, and identifying persons owning, handling, or transacting such funds or assets, a number of measures were introduced to ensure that information of this kind would be identified and promptly reported to the authorities by financial institutions and other reporting entities. To receive such reports, and to process, analyze, and forward that information to the most appropriate investigative body, governments were called upon to create dedicated, specialized, central entities for this purpose—entities described as financial intelligence units (FIUs).

The establishment of an operational FIU that effectively performs the abovementioned core functions is formally required by the FATF and other global standard setters and is also a condition of becoming an Egmont Group member.[3]

FIUs are now widely established and are critical elements in the process of identifying suspicious transactions and assets, and corroborating and elaborating such intelligence/information through access to other state information resources (law enforcement information, identity document information, tax information, property and corporate registries, and so forth) and additional financial information. Once analyzed, and if there are reasons to suspect money laundering or financing of terrorism, the relevant information held by the FIU is disseminated to designated investigative and/or prosecutorial authorities for investigation and prosecution and, if appropriate, for freezing or seizing and, later on, confiscation of the illicit funds.

The Power to Postpone Suspicious Transactions

Terminology

There is no internationally recognized legal definition of the FIU power to postpone a suspicious transaction; therefore, a comparison with similar measures taken by other competent authorities is needed in order to define this term. The FIU order to postpone a suspicious transaction is similar to freezing and seizure, defined in several international conventions as "temporary measures prohibiting the transfer, destruction, conversion, disposition or movement of property or temporarily assuming custody or control of property on the basis of an order issued by court or other competent authority."[4] The term "freezing and seizure" will therefore be used in this chapter only to describe provisional measures issued by judicial, prosecutorial, or law enforcement authorities.

As synonyms for the FIU power to postpone suspicious transactions, some jurisdictions and the Warsaw Convention also use the terms "blocking," "suspending a transaction," and "withholding consent to a transaction going ahead."[5] In this chapter, the terms "FIU postponement of suspicious transaction(s)" and "FIU postponement power" are used synonymously with "freezing and seizure." The term includes the postponement of individual and multiple transactions, as well as attempted and future transactions; that is, those not yet attempted or ordered.

Background

Most FIUs were given the power to postpone suspicious transactions together with other powers at the time of their establishment. This power was historically developed in response to a number of practical problems:

- FIUs receive suspicious transaction reports (STRs) and, in many instances, other types of reports, from financial institutions and designated nonfinancial businesses and professions (DNFBPs[6]). In some cases, a delay in carrying out a full analysis and making a decision as to whether the transaction and related information should be disseminated to law enforcement might result in the reported suspicious transaction being completed, with the possibility that in some instances the funds might be lost for confiscation purposes. Empowering FIUs to order a limited-time postponement of such transactions can prevent the funds from being dissipated or absconded and provides the FIU with additional time to determine whether a transaction is likely related to criminal activity. Before taking a decision regarding postponement, most FIUs, in addition to establishing the required level of suspicion, usually also take into account other circumstances related to the reported transaction and person(s) involved in that transaction. Such circumstances may include the prohibition of "tipping off," and measures that could be taken by the law enforcement authorities or prosecutors.
- Quick access to financial information, or information on assets held by criminals, can be key to successful preventive and repressive measures and, ultimately, for disrupting their networks and unlawful activities. In many jurisdictions FIUs have access to such information more readily than other public authorities. By exchanging such information with the competent domestic and foreign authorities, FIUs can help speed up procedures of restraint, seizure, freezing, and confiscation, targeting proceeds of crime or assets belonging to criminal networks, terrorists, and terrorist organizations.

After the September 11, 2001, terrorist attacks and adoption of the FATF Nine Special Recommendations on Terrorist Financing, FIU mandates were broadened by extending the reporting obligations to the FIU also of transactions suspected of being related to the financing of terrorism. This was supported by the Egmont Group, which in 2004 incorporated countering financing of terrorism as one of the FIU's core functions in the Egmont FIU definition. In implementing the new standards, several jurisdictions extended the FIU power to postpone transactions to include transactions that might be related to financing of terrorism. Some jurisdictions have gone even farther, and in implementing United Nations (UN) Security Council Resolutions related to terrorism, have specifically empowered FIUs to block funds owned or controlled by persons and entities included in UN and/or other regional or national terrorist lists.[7]

The Rationale for the Postponement of Transactions

The FIU power to postpone suspicious transactions is not regulated by FATF or other global international standards, yet it is closely related to the implementation of the following two FATF Recommendations:

- Recommendation 20–Reporting of suspicious and attempted suspicious transactions

One of the reasons for the requirement to report suspicious transactions is to bring to the attention of competent authorities the existence of suspicious assets and transactions involving such funds, and the identity of the owners and/or persons transacting such funds. In addition, it is intended that the public authorities be able to restrain, and ultimately confiscate, illicit assets. It is essential, therefore, that there be sufficient time available in which the FIU and other public authorities can carry out their analysis and other mandated functions.

- Recommendation 4–Confiscation and provisional measures

Countries are required to create a legal framework for freezing or seizing and confiscation measures and to ensure that public authorities have the capacity to act effectively to achieve those purposes. The exercise of those powers is almost always judicially supervised, and depending on the countries' legal systems and required level of suspicion, it can usually take some time for investigative or prosecutorial bodies to freeze an account or to obtain the necessary restraining orders from the courts.

When a financial institution or other reporting entity discerns that a client transaction or proposed transaction gives rise to suspicion that the funds or assets may involve the proceeds of crime and/or constitute money laundering or may be related to terrorist financing, it is required to report its suspicions to the FIU. The nature of many transactions, and the electronic mechanisms for conducting and completing them, means that there may be very little time available to a reporting entity to alert the FIU, which in turn needs to inform the authorities responsible to initiate the process for obtaining a restraining order.

In some circumstances, such as with transactions carried out within the same financial institution or group (for example, the transfer of funds from one account to another account of the same or related account holder), the transactions could be reversed, or the funds involved in transactions remain available for restraint. In other instances, however, transactions may not be easily reversible, and/or the funds or assets may be quickly dissipated, hidden, or transferred (for example, a large cash withdrawal, a wire transfer out of the country, or purchase of easily portable assets such as gold bullion or high-value jewellery or precious stones).

In practice, the postponement of transactions is workable only if STRs and/ or other reports are sent to the FIU before the execution of a related transaction. This is also the approach taken by both regional instruments (the Third European Union Directive and the Warsaw Convention), which imply an a priori reporting, yet allow for exceptions. The practice has also shown that due to the nature of transactions or time needed for a reporting entity to analyze a transaction and justify the suspicion, the vast majority of suspicious transactions are reported to the FIUs only after they have been carried out. Nevertheless, there is a clear international requirement to report attempted suspicious transactions, and some reporting entities, in fact, do report such transactions as well as suspicious transactions with funds and other assets that are still under their control or disposal.

To be able to address these circumstances, a substantial number of jurisdictions have included in the mandates of their FIUs the explicit authority to order reporting entities to postpone, for a certain period of time, if circumstances warrant, the completion of transactions that are suspected of involving the proceeds of crime or terrorist financing. In some jurisdictions this is done implicitly by authorizing the reporting entities to postpone suspicious transactions until they receive a response or consent from the FIU.[8]

Among FIU practitioners, there is no common view as to the applicability, desirability, or utility of having a system that envisages the FIU's power to postpone suspicious transactions. The following arguments are usually put forward in support of their different views in this regard.

Advantages

- **Operational advantage of FIU in the AML supply chain.** FIUs are the "first line of defense" in the anti-money laundering/countering financing of terrorism regime in that they receive suspicious transaction reports directly from financial institutions and DNFBPs. Thus, they may be in a position to temporarily halt the flow of illegal proceeds before they move beyond the reach of national judicial and prosecutorial authorities and can thus facilitate the freezing or seizure of illicit profits or terrorists' funds, which may be subject to confiscation.
- **Easy accessibility of information.** The FIU, because of the broad range of information to which it has or should have access, is normally well equipped to

conduct the analyses necessary to determine whether there are adequate grounds to suspect money laundering or terrorism financing. If so, the FIU should disseminate the relevant information to law enforcement and prosecutorial bodies, and may also postpone a transaction with suspected proceeds of crime, if so authorized.

- **Coordination.** The FIU acts as a bridge between reporting entities and law enforcement or prosecutorial authorities and is therefore well positioned to communicate with and facilitate the tasks of both, including those that are aimed at securing the suspected assets that might be subject to confiscation.

Disadvantages

- **Risk of "tipping off."** Postponement of suspicious transactions carries a high risk of "tipping off" the subject (owner or conductor of the transaction) under scrutiny and suspicion, thereby possibly triggering the flight of individuals involved in the laundering activity, or the removal of other, as yet undetected, funds or assets.
- **Postponement is not part of FIU core functions.** Postponement is a resource-intensive executive action that does not fit well with the FIU's intelligence function, and can divert FIU resources to those administrative or executive functions at the expense of the FIU's analytic role.
- **Risk of losing focus.** The urgent and strong focus on individual transactions inherent in the postponement process shrinks the vision of the FIU, and may result in the systematic concentration on smaller, single event, or single perpetrator cases rather than searching for much larger, and ongoing, network cases that some FIUs have found to be the modus operandi of significant criminal organizations.
- **Disruption of normal course of business.** Postponement disrupts the flow of financial transactions and may interfere with the ability of individuals to conduct what may be legitimate financial activities. It is also perceived as a breach of contractual relationship between the reporting entity and its client, which in some cases has already led to civil litigation.
- **Protection of fundamental rights of client or suspect.** If the duration of postponement is too long, the FIU should be obliged to ensure that the right to appeal and other fundamental rights of the client or suspect and other persons affected by the postponement are protected. This raises a delicate question of sharing at least some FIU data with the client or suspect.

International/Regional Standards

As mentioned, there are no global international standards regulating FIU power to postpone transactions. At a regional level, the Warsaw Convention (2005) is the most important international instrument dealing explicitly with the FIU power to postpone a suspicious transaction.[9] Article 14 of the Warsaw Convention requires member states to introduce this measure at the national level, although

---

Box 2.1

Articles 14 and 47 of the Warsaw Convention

Article 14–Postponement of domestic suspicious transactions

Each Party shall adopt such legislative and other measures as may be necessary to permit urgent action to be taken by the FIU or, as appropriate, by any other competent authorities or body, when there is a suspicion that a transaction is related to money laundering, to suspend or withhold consent to a transaction going ahead in order to analyze the transaction and confirm the suspicion. Each party may restrict such a measure to cases where a suspicious transaction report has been submitted. The maximum duration of any suspension or withholding of consent to a transaction shall be subject to any relevant provisions in national law.

Article 47–International co-operation for postponement of suspicious transactions

1. Each Party shall adopt such legislative or other measures as may be necessary to permit urgent action to be initiated by a FIU, at the request of a foreign FIU, to suspend or withhold consent to a transaction going ahead for such periods and depending on the same conditions as apply in its domestic law in respect of the postponement of transactions.
2. The action referred to in paragraph 1 shall be taken where the requested FIU is satisfied, upon justification by the requesting FIU, that:
   a. the transaction is related to money laundering; and
   b. the transaction would have been suspended, or consent to the transaction going ahead would have been withheld, if the transaction had been the subject of a domestic suspicious transaction report.

Note: FIU = Financial Intelligence Unit

---

it permits them to assign this power to the FIU or any other competent authority or body. Article 47 of the Convention regulates the use of postponement power on behalf of a foreign FIU. When receiving such a request, the requested FIU may represent the authority responsible for making a decision on postponement or just serve as the point of contact for the foreign requesting FIU. In this regard, Article 52 of the Warsaw Convention allows member states to reserve their right not to apply the provisions of Article 47. The text of both articles is provided in box 2.1.

In Europe, European Union Directive 2005/60/EC on the Prevention of the Use of the Financial System for the Purpose of Money Laundering and Terrorist Financing (Third EU AML/CFT Directive) also contains provisions dealing with the suspension of suspicious transactions. Article 24 of the Directive requires reporting entities to refrain from carrying out transactions suspected of being related to money laundering or terrorist financing until they have informed the FIU. According to this provision, instructions may be given not to

Box 2.2

Paragraph 1 of Article 24 of the Third EU AML/CFT Directive

Article 24

1. Member States shall require the institutions and persons covered by this Directive to refrain from carrying out transactions which they know or suspect to be related to money laundering or terrorist financing until they have completed the necessary action in accordance with Article 22(1) (a).ᵃ In conformity with the legislation of the Member States, instructions may be given not to carry out the transaction.

Note: AML/CFT = anti-money laundering/countering financing of terrorism, EU = European Union, FIU = Financial Intelligence Unit.
a. Article 22 (1) (a) states: "Member states shall require the institutions and persons covered by this Directive, and where applicable their directors and employees, to cooperate fully: (a) by promptly informing the FIU, on their own initiative, where the institution or person covered by this Directive knows, suspects or has reasonable grounds to suspect that money laundering or terrorist financing is being or has been committed or attempted."

carry out the transaction. The Directive does not provide any further guidance as to which body should be empowered to give such instructions and leaves this entirely to the member states. The text of paragraph 1 of Article 24 is provided in box 2.2.

In March 2012, the European Union Commission announced a proposal for a new Directive on the freezing and confiscation of proceeds of crime in the European Union (EU).¹⁰ The draft Directive recognizes that the existing confiscation and freezing regimes are not fully effective, and lays down minimum rules for member states with respect to freezing and confiscation of criminal assets through direct confiscation, value confiscation, extended confiscation, nonconviction-based confiscation (in limited circumstances), and third-party confiscation.¹¹ Although the draft Directive intends to regulate the judicial freezing or confiscation powers and not the FIU postponement power, it addresses the same gap in the current freezing or confiscation procedures that some FIU practitioners identified as being one of the initial reasons for giving the postponement power to the FIUs.

The draft Directive envisages a new requirement related to the use of freezing powers in urgent cases in order to prevent asset dissipation in situations where waiting for an order issued by a court would jeopardize the possibilities of freezing or seizing. To that end, paragraph 2 of Article 7 of the draft Directive requires member states to have in place measures to ensure that assets in danger of being dissipated, hidden, or transferred out of their jurisdiction can be frozen immediately by the competent authorities, prior to seeking a court order or pending its request. In addition, the proposed Article 8 requires member states to introduce all the necessary safeguards to ensure that the rights of persons affected by provisional measures are effectively protected. The text of both draft articles is provided in box 2.3.

Box 2.3

Article 7 and Paragraphs 1 and 2 of Article 8 of the Draft EU Directive on the Freezing and Confiscation of Proceeds of Crime in the European Union

Article 7–Freezing

1. Each Member State shall take the necessary measures to enable it to freeze property in danger of being dissipated, hidden or transferred out of the jurisdiction with a view to possible later confiscation. Such measures shall be ordered by a court.
2. Each Member State shall take the necessary measures to enable its competent authorities to immediately freeze property when there is a high risk of dissipation, hiding or transfer of that property before a court's decision. Such measures shall be confirmed by a court as soon as possible.

Article 8–Safeguards

1. Each Member State shall take the necessary measures to ensure that the persons affected by the measures provided for under this Directive have the right to an effective remedy and that suspects have the right to a fair trial, in order to preserve their rights.
2. Each Member State shall take the necessary measures to ensure that reasons are given for any decision to freeze property, that the decision is communicated to the person affected as soon as possible after its execution and that it remains in force only for as long as it is necessary to preserve the property with a view to future confiscation. Each Member State shall provide for the effective possibility to appeal against the decision to freeze by the persons whose property is affected before a court at any time before a decision on confiscation is taken. Frozen property which is not subsequently confiscated shall be returned immediately to its legitimate owner.

Note: EU = European Union.

As can be seen, the European standards require jurisdictions to protect fundamental rights, including (a) the right to property, (b) presumption of innocence and right of defense, (c) the right to an effective judicial remedy before a court and the right to be informed on how to exercise it, and (d) the right to protection of personal data. According to the European Court of Human Rights jurisprudence, fundamental rights, such as the right to property, can be subject to certain restrictions provided that the following conditions are met:

- Restrictions should be regulated in law.
- Restrictions should be necessary (subject to the principle of proportionality).
- Restrictions should meet objectives of general interest or the need to protect the rights and freedoms of others, as in the prevention of money laundering and terrorist financing.[12]

What Has Been the Experience?

For a decade or longer the mandates of a substantial number of FIUs have included the power to postpone suspicious transactions. Although there has been some discussion of the utility and effectiveness of that tool, there has been very little documented experience available to inform such consideration. As a consequence, discussions have been based largely on theoretical or ideological positions, often relying on anecdotal information to support one or the other position of the parties to such, mainly informal, consideration of the questions. There has been a clear lack of precise and reliable information at hand as to the nature and extent of the legal arrangements developed to empower FIUs in this regard. Similarly, there has been no documented information available as to the circumstances, conditions, and challenges inherent in the use of such a power, or about the extent and frequency of its use or the results flowing from that use.

The Egmont Group Biennial Census of 2010 included a question about this subject, and the results confirmed that at least 65 Egmont member FIUs have the power to postpone suspicious transactions. In response to a growing demand for reliable information about the manner and conditions of the use of that power, and the extent and frequency of its use by those FIUs so empowered, the Egmont Group and the World Bank decided in 2011 to undertake a joint study, including a survey, to collect more information in this regard.

This study has generated a lot of information about practices, procedures, and conditions of use, related to the power of FIUs to postpone transactions. It has also raised a number of questions about some of those practices, and about the puzzling revelation that even among the FIU population that has the power to postpone transactions, there are a surprising number of FIUs that do not use the power at all, or use it only rarely. These questions could not be answered and interpreted reliably in this report because they fell outside its scope, and more research would be needed to do so.

The complete report on the survey is contained in appendix A. Highlights include the following:

- The study was based on the survey responses of 88 FIUs that participated in the study. Of that number, 26 FIUs (30 percent) indicated that they did not have the power to postpone transactions and 62 FIUs (70 percent) indicated that they do. Of the 62 FIUs that have the power to postpone, 17 had not used the power in the three-year period covered by the study, and 10 had used it only infrequently, one to three times during the three-year period. A small handful of FIUs account for the lion's share of the postponement activity reported in the study.
- The specific legal arrangements governing the postponement power vary greatly among FIUs, and despite the fact that postponement is a coercive measure, there are a small number of FIUs that have no explicit legal basis for postponing suspicious transactions.

- The application of the postponement power to different categories of offenses also raises some potentially conflicting issues. While most of the FIUs can apply this power to terrorist financing, money laundering, and/or related predicate offenses, some FIUs can also apply it to funds or assets related to violations (administrative offenses) that are not classified as crimes. Furthermore, a substantial number of FIUs can use their postponement power in the freezing process under the UN Security Resolutions related to terrorism, which in most cases seem to be inconsistent with the requirements under these resolutions.

- Postponement of transactions is typically a short-term, interim measure intended to provide time for the FIU to complete its assessment as to whether there are grounds to suspect that the funds or assets involved are proceeds from criminal activity or related to terrorist financing, and for the competent authorities to initiate freezing and restraint measures, when appropriate. There is, however, a wide range in the maximum duration period of postponements among jurisdictions. Lengthy durations of postponement orders, (sometimes as long as six months or longer), based only on what at the outset is likely to be superficial analysis and suspicion, may cause unwarranted hardship and financial loss to the owners of the funds or assets in question. Moreover, most jurisdictions have not provided the authority to lift postponement orders before their expiry date, even if, after the FIU analysis, the transactions in question are found not to be suspicious.

- The triggers for the use of the power vary from one jurisdiction to another, and there is variation in the factors that are considered in making a determination to order a postponement. Many FIUs issue a postponement order based on an STR from a reporting entity, but in many instances they may also do so on the basis of requests from the reporting entity, and in some instances based on requests from law enforcement or prosecutorial authorities. This raises additional concerns about the independence of the FIU, and the possibility that law enforcement and prosecutors may be improperly using the FIU as a tool to circumvent laws governing the freezing and seizing of suspect assets.

- There is also variation in the scope of the application of the postponement power to different, related or unrelated, transactions or accounts that are identified in additional institutions in the course of the analysis of the suspicious transaction(s) that may have sparked the analysis. It is not always clear that the risk of flight or dissipation of funds or assets is a key factor in the decision as to whether or not transactions should be postponed, and whether there is reason to freeze all transactions on any and all accounts in the name of or under the control of a suspect.

- The rights of appeal and recourse by parties whose funds or transactions have been postponed are often not clearly set out or readily accessible by those parties.

- The findings of the study also indicate weak performance by FIUs in follow-up to postponement orders to determine the outcome, and there appear to be

poorly developed habits of collecting and retaining statistical data on postponements and follow-on activity and outcomes. The data on outcomes of
postponements are scant, because only a small fraction of respondent FIUs
provided this kind of information, but the reported data reflect relatively low
values of funds subject to final confiscation.
• The infrequent use, or nonuse, of the power raises puzzling questions as to what
  lies behind it. Is it inexperience and lack of knowledge? Is it cumbersome or
  troublesome to use? Is it ineffective in producing worthwhile results? Or is it
  something else? As mentioned, the data from this study were not sufficient or
  reliable enough to answer these questions.

Notes

1. The FATF is an intergovernmental body established by the ministers of its member
   jurisdictions. The objectives of the FATF are to set standards and promote effective
   implementation of legal, regulatory, and operational measures for combating money
   laundering, terrorist financing, and other related threats to the integrity of the international financial system. See more at http://www.fatf-gafi.org/pages/aboutus/.

2. The last revision of FATF Recommendations was promulgated in February 2012,
   when the amended recommendations were adopted and published by the FATF (see
   http://www.fatf-gafi.org/topics/fatfrecommendations/documents/fatfrecommenda-
   tions2012.html). This chapter refers only to the 40 FATF Recommendations that are
   currently in force.

3. FATF Recommendation 29 requires countries to "establish a FIU that serves as a
   national centre for the receipt and analysis of: (a) suspicious transaction reports; and
   (b) other information relevant to money laundering, associated predicate offences and
   terrorist financing, and for the dissemination of the results of that analysis. The FIU
   should be able to obtain additional information from reporting entities, and should
   have access on a timely basis to the financial, administrative and law enforcement
   information that it requires to undertake its functions properly." Similar but less
   detailed provisions related to the establishment of FIUs are also contained in Article
   14 of the UNCAC and Article 7 of the Palermo Convention.

4. See Article 1 of the Warsaw Convention, Article 2 of the Palermo Convention, and
   Article 2 of the UNCAC.

5. IMF and World Bank, "Financial Intelligence Units–An Overview," Washington, DC,
   2004, p. 75. See also Article 14 of the Warsaw Convention.

6. The list of DNFBPs include, subject to certain conditions, the following entities:
   (a) casinos; (b) real estate agents; (c) dealers in precious metals and precious stones;
   (d) lawyers, notaries, other independent legal professionals, and accountants; and
   (e) trusts and company service providers.

7. S/RES/1267(1999), its successor resolutions, and S/RES/1373(2011).

8. The postponement mechanisms that are only executed by the reporting entities
   themselves are highly controversial, because the postponement of transactions is by
   nature a coercive and repressive measure that should fall under the responsibility of a
   public authority. Such mechanisms may also negatively affect the reporting of STRs.

9. By May 1, 2012, the Warsaw Convention had been ratified by 22 jurisdictions and signed by an additional 12 jurisdictions. The FATF in its revised Recommendation 36 (International Instruments) is encouraging countries to ratify and implement the Warsaw Convention.

10. The European Commission Proposal for a Directive of the European Parliament and of the Council on the freezing and confiscation of proceeds of crime in the European Union, COM (2012) 85 final, Brussels, 12.3.2012. See http://eur-lex.europa.eu/LexUriServ/LexUriServ.do?uri=COM:2012:0085:FIN:EN:PDF.

11. Ibid., pp. 3 and 14.

12. Ibid., p. 12.

CHAPTER 3

Recommendations

The recommendations in this chapter highlight issues identified during the World Bank–Egmont Group study and are not intended to advocate that all Financial Intelligence Units (FIUs) should have or acquire the power to postpone transactions. In the course of reviewing and analyzing the responses to the survey questionnaire, the authors identified a number of areas in which there appear to be issues that FIUs might wish to consider for possible improvements, refinements, or restraints in the way the power is established and/or used.

The recommendations made here are intended to provide perspective and guidance on sound practice in respect of a number of issues that arise from the study. They are available to FIUs that want to strengthen their use of this power, and to those that might want to acquire and apply the power to postpone transactions. It is recognized that there will always be variations from one jurisdiction to another, owing to particular practices and procedures in any given jurisdiction.[1] However, the recommendations here provide advice as to the nature, scope, and application of powers and capacities that form the basis of a solid and effective regime for postponement of suspicious transactions.

The recommendations are organized into two sections:

- *Legal/Policy Recommendations*: This section provides legal and policy recommendations related to selected legal aspects of the FIU postponement power and aims to assist policy makers in establishing effective legal mechanisms governing the postponement power.
- *Operational Recommendations*: This section presents operational guidance that aims to facilitate effective and more coordinated use of this power between FIUs and other competent authorities and among FIUs.

The introductory paragraph(s) under each recommendation present the findings of the study and include footnotes referencing the relevant part of the Report in appendix A. The following paragraphs provide a link with the international standards, if applicable, and arguments supporting the recommendation.

Legal/Policy Recommendations

Provide an explicit legal basis for the FIU power to postpone suspicious transactions, regulating all relevant aspects of this power.

The World Bank–Egmont Group survey shows that while in most jurisdictions the FIUs have an explicit statutory basis for the authority to postpone suspicious transactions, there are a small number of FIUs (all in common law jurisdictions) without such an explicit legal basis. The survey also shows that in several jurisdictions, many important aspects of the FIU power to postpone suspicious transactions are insufficiently or not at all regulated in the legislation.[2]

The FIU power to postpone suspicious transactions is a coercive measure that affects client's or suspect's rights, reporting entity obligations, and the normal conduct of business and transactions. It is recommended that jurisdictions ensure that the authority to postpone a suspicious transaction is explicitly provided in the anti-money laundering/countering financing of terrorism or other laws. Like with other provisional measures of the same nature (seizure and freezing), and in line with the principle of legality, the jurisdictions should consider regulating all relevant elements of the FIU postponement power, including the following:

- Minimum factors that need to be present to warrant a postponement
- Right to be notified about the postponement and right of appeal, if applicable
- Maximum duration
- International postponement of suspicious transactions, if applicable
- Cancellation of the postponement order prior to its expiration
- Form and content of the postponement order
- Liability for damages.

Ensure that the postponement decision remains with the FIU.

In a significant number of jurisdictions, requests from law enforcement authorities, other public authorities, and reporting entities are important factors that can trigger the use of FIU postponement power. Moreover, in some of these jurisdictions the level of suspicion raised outside the FIU is the prevailing and mandatory factor in this context.[3] This aspect can potentially affect the capacity of an FIU to fulfill its mandate in regard to this power independently and in line with FIU international standards.

According to Financial Action Task Force (FATF) Recommendation 29 and the related Interpretative Note, the FIU should be operationally independent and autonomous, meaning that the FIU should have the authority and capacity to carry out its functions freely. The same standards require that when the FIU receives a request from law enforcement or other competent authorities, the decision on conducting analysis and/or dissemination of information should still remain with the FIU.

While the power to postpone transactions is not part of the FIU's core functions (receiving, analyzing, requesting, and disseminating information), it is closely related to these functions. It would therefore seem logical to use the same approach regarding the FIU independence and autonomy that applies to the FIU's core functions to the FIU power to postpone suspicious transactions. It is recommended that the FIU have an independent right to make its own analysis of data and take a decision regarding the use of this measure in all circumstances, irrespective of whether it is considering issuing the postponement order on the basis of its own suspicion, a reported transaction, or on behalf of another competent authority, domestic or foreign.

Identify the minimum requisite conditions that would have to be present for the FIU to exercise its power to postpone suspicious transactions.

The survey shows that in some jurisdictions, FIUs can postpone a transaction only if they have received a request or a suspicious transaction report from the reporting entity or a request from the competent judicial or law enforcement authority. These FIUs are usually not in a position to assess whether other conditions related to the level of suspicion or the risks of losing suspected funds exist.[4]

In most jurisdictions, the legislation requires that certain conditions are met in order to issue a seizing or freezing order. These provisional measures are carried out by judicial and/or prosecutorial or law enforcement authorities and are subject to establishing a certain level of suspicion and other conditions that usually apply in criminal procedures concerning the provisional measures. The FIU postponement power is also a provisional measure, and therefore could be subject to similar conditions that can trigger the use of this power. While the procedural requirements may vary from country to country, the legislation should provide for some minimum substantive conditions that must be taken into account by all FIUs when they exercise their power to postpone suspicious transactions.[5] It is recommended that these conditions include the following:

- Reasonable grounds to suspect[6] that a transaction is related to money laundering, associated predicate offenses, or terrorist financing
- Reasonable grounds to suspect that the funds or the conductor or owner of the funds in question might leave the jurisdiction, the funds cannot be monitored, or the money trail might be lost (for example, in case of cash withdrawals).

Both factors should apply simultaneously. Furthermore, it is recommended that the postponement power is used only when it seems likely that the competent judicial, prosecutorial, or law enforcement authorities will initiate a criminal case and will complement the postponement order with a subsequent restraining or freezing order. All these conditions will require FIUs to use the postponement power more cautiously and direct the use of this tool toward the larger goal of freezing or seizure by the relevant authorities so as to prevent postponing every reported or identified suspicious transaction.

Apply the FIU postponement power to transactions related to suspected money laundering, associated predicate offenses, and suspected terrorist financing.

Jurisdictions have different arrangements in place with regard to the use of FIU power to postpone suspicious transactions. While in some jurisdictions the FIUs can only postpone transactions involving funds identified in the reporting entity's or state body's report or request, in others the FIUs can postpone transactions in respect of all funds linked with the suspect, including funds that are not direct or indirect proceeds from crime or instrumentalities. Moreover, in a small number of jurisdictions the FIUs can also postpone transactions with funds that are proceeds from misdemeanors or administrative offenses.[7]

The FIU's main mandate is to deal with transactions and other information relevant to money laundering, associated predicate offenses, and terrorist financing. The FIU should, therefore, consider using the postponement power only in relation to transactions that fall into its mandate. To that end, it is recommended that jurisdictions implement the legislative or other measures to achieve the following:

- If the minimum requisite conditions are met, the FIU should be able to use the postponement power with respect to any identified suspicious transaction, irrespective of the source of information that led to postponement.

The FIU may learn about an attempted or ongoing transaction in different ways, for example, via (a) an STR or Currency Transaction Report (CTR), (b) a request from law enforcement or prosecutorial authorities, (c) information from the AML/CFT supervisory authority, (d) a request or spontaneous information from a foreign FIU, or (e) media or other public sources. With the postponement of transactions, additional time is given to the FIU to collect and analyze data and confirm the initial suspicion, and to the competent judicial or law enforcement authorities to take and implement a decision to seize or freeze the funds in question. When taking a decision as to whether to postpone a suspicious transaction, and in order to meet these objectives, it should not matter how the FIU learned about such suspicious transactions. The source of information should be taken into account only if so required by the procedural rules of the jurisdiction concerned.

- The FIU should consider using the postponement power only to suspend transactions that are related to criminal offenses of money laundering, related predicate offenses, and terrorist financing.

FIUs were created in order to deal with money laundering and terrorist financing, that is, with criminal activities that fall into the category of serious crimes.

Allowing the FIU to use the power to postpone transactions to deal with the violations of law or other offenses outside the AML/CFT mandate (for example, misdemeanors or administrative offenses) is inappropriate.

- The FIU should consider using the postponement power only for transactions regarding property about which there are reasonable grounds to suspect that it has been, or is about to be, laundered or it constitutes the proceeds from, or instrumentalities used in, the commission of money laundering, related predicate offenses, and terrorist financing.

The FATF Recommendations and other international standards require jurisdictions to freeze, seize, and also confiscate property of the corresponding value, yet these measures apply to competent judicial and law enforcement authorities, and not to FIUs. Authorizing FIUs to postpone transactions with legally obtained property would go far beyond its original mandate. It would also give FIUs the authority to make an unqualified judgment that enters into the competences of the competent judicial or law enforcement authorities, since the FIU postponement order would anticipate that these authorities would take a similar measure against the legally obtained property in order to secure the confiscation of property of corresponding value. Since in practice the FIUs usually have little time to decide whether to postpone a suspicious transaction, they may not always be able to distinguish between legally and illegally obtained funds or property. Therefore, it seems logical that FIUs should apply this recommendation only when they know that the transaction is related to illegally obtained funds or property.

Apply the FIU postponement power to transactions conducted at financial institutions and Designated Non-Financial Businesses and Professions (DNFBPs), if the nature of a transaction permits such an action to be taken.

The study indicates that while in most jurisdictions the FIUs are authorized to postpone transactions conducted at all reporting entities (financial institutions and DNFBPs), there are a small number of jurisdictions where the FIUs can only postpone transactions carried out at financial institutions.[8]

Experience has shown that FIUs receive most STRs and other reports from financial institutions and that the vast majority of the postponed transactions also take place in the financial sector. The reasons for the low number of reported STRs and postponement orders issued with regard to transactions conducted by DNFBPs jurisdictions usually include the following: (a) a large number of these transactions are carried out by one-off customers, where the possibility of undertaking customer due diligence and identifying a suspicious transaction is more difficult; and (b) these transactions usually happen immediately, and any interruption of the normal flow of business may increase the risk that the customer would learn about the postponement.

Financial institutions and DNFBPs are both required to take customer due diligence and other measures in order to prevent money laundering and terrorist financing. These measures include promptly reporting to the FIU their suspicions that funds are the proceeds of a criminal activity or are related to terrorist financing.[9] Furthermore, transactions similar to those carried out by DNFBPs are also common in financial institutions (for example, currency exchange and money transfers), yet in most jurisdictions where the FIUs have postponement power, all transactions in financial institutions are subject to possible postponement.

In practice it is possible to postpone at least some suspicious transactions at casinos, and by lawyers, notaries, real estate agents, and other DNFBPs, if their nature allows for such actions to be taken.[10] It is recommended that jurisdictions avoid having double legal standards with regard to the applicability of the postponement power, and permit FIUs to postpone suspicious transactions conducted at all reporting entities.

Ensure that legislation mandates a reasonable maximum duration of the FIU postponement order. Legislation may provide for a longer maximum duration when it is legally or practically irrelevant whether the client or suspect learns about the postponement order, or when the FIU needs to collect information from abroad, but in such cases the fundamental rights of all those concerned must be protected.

The World Bank–Egmont Group survey identifies a significant number of jurisdictions whose laws do not provide for any limits with regard to the maximum duration of the FIU postponement order, and jurisdictions with a longer duration period, where the fundamental rights of persons affected by the measure may not be sufficiently protected. In addition, in several jurisdictions with a longer duration period, the FIUs do not take any measures to avoid "tipping off"[11] the client, suspect, or third persons as to the postponement order.[12]

The duration of the period for which the FIU may postpone a transaction is a very sensitive issue, because jurisdictions must take into account several competing issues when designing their legislation related to the FIU postponement power. These issues include the following:

- The FIU needs sufficient time to analyze the reported suspicion, collect additional data (including from abroad), and disseminate its findings to the competent authority.
- If the FIU postpones a transaction for too long, there is a significant risk that the client or suspect will learn that his or her transaction has been reported as suspicious and has been postponed, and this risk must be effectively mitigated.
- Postponing transactions for a longer period raises questions related to the client's fundamental rights that must be protected.

To achieve the desired objectives while respecting FIU international standards and the rule of law, it is recommended that jurisdictions take into account the following principles:

- Postponement of a suspicious transaction is an interim measure of a preventive nature and should not become a restraint or a punitive measure. The legislation should therefore define a reasonable maximum permitted duration of the FIU postponement order, which should ideally not exceed 72 hours (or three days).[13]

The indicated period might not give the FIU enough time to carry out all its activities, in particular in cases with several suspects and multiple transactions, or when the FIU must obtain information from foreign FIUs. However, this seems to be a reasonable period, during which the reporting entity and/or the FIU might still be able to effectively prevent the postponement coming to the attention of the client or suspect.

- Legislation should determine whether the FIU may renew a postponement order, and if so, for how long and under what conditions. If applicable, all the renewals should be included in the maximum duration of the postponement order.
- Simultaneous postponements done by the reporting entity[14] and FIU should count as one in terms of maximum permitted duration and associated risk of tipping off.
- When in a particular jurisdiction the reporting entities and/or FIU are not prohibited from informing the client or suspect about the FIU postponement order due to its legal system or operational arrangements, or the FIU needs to obtain data from abroad, the legislation may allow for a longer postponement period. In such cases the fundamental rights of all those affected by the postponement order should be taken into account. These should include the right to be informed about the postponement, the right to be represented by a lawyer, the obligation to communicate any decision affecting property, and to have the possibility to appeal such decision.

If the duration of a postponement order is longer than suggested above, there is a very high risk that the client or suspect will learn that his or her transaction has been reported as suspicious and postponed. A lengthy period of postponement also interferes more rigorously with the property and other fundamental rights of the client or suspect and other persons who might be affected by the postponement (for example, bona fide third parties). It is recommended that jurisdictions ensure that the fundamental rights of all those concerned are protected, including the right to be notified about the proceedings and the right to appeal the postponement order. There should be a clear and publicly known procedure in place dealing with the above-mentioned rights; general provisions allowing persons affected by the decisions of a competent state authority to appeal such decisions are not deemed sufficient.

Furthermore, granting a right to appeal an FIU's postponement order raises a range of questions that must be answered in legislation. The latter should clearly identify who is required to notify the client, suspect, or other persons of the postponement and what information should be disclosed in the course of these legal proceedings. Caution is in order: relying on intelligence as the chief touch-stone for FIU decisions about whether and when to postpone a suspicious trans-action creates a wide opening for divergent interpretations and vulnerabilities to parties with an interest in getting access to FIU confidential information.

More important, this could also be seen as taking the FIU out of its core mandate as an intelligence gatherer and placing it in the position of having to justify its decision and possibly challenge the information obtained. Allowing a long duration of the FIU postponement power may therefore require the FIUs to deal with all the above-mentioned issues and, if so, it is likely that this will undermine the performance of their core functions.

Introduce legal provisions allowing the FIU to cancel a postponement order before its expiry date, when the reasons for the postponement cease to exist.

The World Bank–Egmont Group survey shows that in several jurisdictions the FIUs are not authorized to cancel their postponement orders before the expiry date, even if the FIUs' anaylsis leads to abandoning the initial suspicion that led to postponement.[15]

It is therefore recommended that FIUs be legally authorized to lift a post-ponement order as soon as it is determined that the initial suspicion has not been confirmed or that certain other conditions are met. Such conditions may include the following:

- There is no longer a risk that the funds, the client, or the suspect will flee the jurisdiction.
- The FIU can no longer effectively mitigate the risk of a client or suspect being alerted about the postponement order.
- A formal restraining order or freezing order has been issued by competent authorities.
- The legal origin of funds in question has been proven.
- Investigation into the person or transaction has ceased.

Allowing an FIU to cancel its postponement order before its expiry date not only diminishes the risk of any tipping off related to the reported suspicious transaction but also protects the right to property and other contractual rights and reduces the potential losses of all concerned. To achieve these goals, it is recommended that the FIU notify the reporting entity of its decision as soon as possible.

Ensure that the reporting entities, the FIU, and their representatives are protected by law from criminal and civil liability for any possible damage caused due to the postponed transaction, if the postponement was carried out lawfully and in good faith.

According to the survey, in the majority of jurisdictions the FIUs and their staff involved in the postponement decision are shielded from liability for losses suffered by the client or suspect or bona fide third party. However, explicit legal provisions for such immunity exist only in some jurisdictions, while in others no protection is provided or the immunity is provided under the general indemnity for public officials acting in good faith.[16]

FATF Recommendation 21 requires countries to exclude the reporting entities, their directors, officers, and employees from criminal and civil liability for breach of any restriction on disclosure of information, if they report the suspicious transaction in good faith to the FIU. While this international standard does not apply to postponement orders, it would make sense to use a similar approach when the reporting entities and their representatives—acting in good faith—postpone a suspicious transaction on the basis of law or a postponement order issued by the FIU.

In this regard, it is recommended that the reporting entities, the FIU, and their representatives be treated in the same manner. They should enjoy an equal level of protection when they are engaged in issuing or implementing a postponement order. Jurisdictions should therefore consider including in their legislation general or specific immunity provisions for the reporting entities' and FIU's lawful actions related to the postponing of transactions, if they are taken in good faith.

Such immunity provisions should not exclude the obligation of jurisdictions to foresee judicial remedies for a client or suspect and for other persons who suffered losses, in a similar manner that apply to losses caused by provisional measures carried out by the competent judicial or law enforcement authorities.

Avoid using the FIU power to postpone transactions in the freezing process under the UN Security Council Resolutions related to terrorism, if there is no regulated complementary freezing procedure carried out by another competent authority.

The survey shows that in a significant number of jurisdictions, the FIUs use their power to postpone suspicious transactions in order to meet the requirements under the freezing mechanisms envisaged by the United Nations Security Council (UNSC) Resolutions related to terrorism. In only a few of these jurisdictions is the FIU postponement of transactions related to persons listed under these resolutions supplemented within a short period of time with an administrative freezing procedure that does not rely on criminal standards.[17]

The UNSC Resolutions related to terrorism require countries to, among other things, freeze the funds of persons and entities designated by the UN

Al-Qaida and Taliban Sanctions Committee under Resolution 1267 and its successor resolutions, or designated by countries themselves pursuant to Resolution 1373. According to FATF Recommendation 5 and a related Interpretative Note, the freezing obligation applies to all natural and legal persons within the country and to all funds that are owned (wholly or jointly; directly or indirectly) or controlled by the designated persons; funds derived or generated from such funds; and funds of persons acting on behalf of, or at the direction of, designated persons. The freezing mechanism therefore applies to all funds, even if they were obtained lawfully, and not just to those that can be tied to a particular terrorist act, plot, or threat. Furthermore, the above-mentioned resolutions explicitly state that the freezing measures should not be reliant upon criminal standards[18] and should be in force until a particular person is delisted from the list of designated persons.

It is clear from the above that using the FIU postponement power in the freezing process under the UNSC Resolutions seems to be:

- Inconsistent with the requirements under the UNSC resolutions (indefinite freezing; referring to all legal and natural persons and not just to reporting entities; requiring the freezing of all property, not reliant upon criminal standards)
- Inconsistent with the primary role of FIUs (dealing with information related to terrorist financing, money laundering, and related predicate offenses)
- Noncompliant with Articles 14 and 47 of the Warsaw Convention[19]
- Ineffective, since it is unlikely that in cases where the FIUs use their postponement power in order to implement the UNSC resolutions, they are also able to provide any meaningful evidence (in addition to noting that a suspect is a designated person), which is normally needed in a criminal procedure in order to replace their postponement orders with a freezing or seizing order.

Therefore, ideally, the FIUs should not be involved in the freezing process under the UNSC resolutions.

It is, however, acknowledged that some FIUs are required to play an active role in this process due to the legislative and/or other operational arrangements imposed in their jurisdictions. In these circumstances it is recommended that the use of FIU postponement power be subject to the following conditions:

- The FIU postponement order should remain strictly a temporary measure that is used in the same manner as recommended above (explicit provision in the law, minimum triggers, reasonable postponement period, application to ongoing transactions, and so forth). This is necessary to avoid the risk of having two different ways of carrying out the postponement power, and also to ensure that the FIUs use their postponement power only in urgent cases in order to prevent asset dissipation in situations where waiting for an order issued by a competent authority would jeopardize the possibilities of freezing.

- Legislation should provide a complementary administrative (noncriminal) freezing procedure in compliance with the above-mentioned UNSC resolutions and FATF Recommendation 5.

Introduce legal provisions that will:

- **Require FIUs to issue a written postponement order, at least in cases where a longer postponement period is feasible**
- **Allow the FIU to issue an oral postponement order in urgent cases, when the nature of a transaction does not give the FIU sufficient time to issue a written order in a timely manner.**

In several jurisdictions, FIUs are only allowed to issue a postponement order in written form, with the exception of some of those FIUs that are only empowered to give or withhold their permission for a suspicious transaction to be carried out.[20]

It is important that the FIU, as a matter of principle, be obliged to issue a written postponement order (or a written decision), at least in cases where the legislation allows for a longer postponement period. As mentioned, the postponement of suspicious transactions is a coercive measure that affects property and other contractual rights. The written form is needed to ensure effective protection of the fundamental rights of the client or suspect and all those concerned. To that effect, it is also recommended that the postponement order contain some minimum data, such as, for example, the legal basis for postponement, the name and address of the reporting entity, identification data related to the client or suspect and transaction, and information on whether there is a right to appeal the postponement order. In this regard, a model template is provided in appendix D, which the FIUs might wish to use as guidance.

Furthermore, practice has shown that in urgent cases there is an obvious need for FIUs to act quickly to prevent suspicious transactions being completed, especially in cases in which the funds involved could be transferred beyond the reach of the competent authorities. It is recommended that in such urgent circumstances the FIUs have the legal authority to issue an oral postponement order that should be supplemented with a written order shortly afterward.

Consider adopting laws allowing:

- **FIUs to request a foreign FIU to postpone a suspicious transaction on its behalf**
- **FIUs to postpone a suspicious transaction at the request of a foreign FIU.[21]**

Not long after the adoption of the Warsaw Convention in 2005, countries began regulating the FIU postponement power at the international level. Despite the fact that the Warsaw Convention allows countries to make a reservation or declaration with regard to the international cooperation for postponement of

transactions, only a few countries have done so.[22] Moreover, the World Bank–
Egmont Group survey shows that more than 60 percent of FIUs with the power
to postpone suspicious transactions can request a foreign FIU to issue a postponement order on their behalf and issue a postponement order at the request
of a foreign FIU. However, in a significant number of jurisdictions, the FIU
cooperation related to the postponement of transactions is not clearly regulated
in the legislation, and it has rarely been applied in practice.[23]

Comprehensive and effective AML/CFT regimes must allow for FIU-to-FIU
exchange of information and cooperation in other areas of common interest.
This is an important tool in the fight against transnational money laundering and
terrorism financing. It is, in fact, so significant that the authority to exchange
information with other FIUs is an element of the international standard for
FIUs.[24] In addition, authority and willingness to engage in such exchanges are
part of the Egmont definition of an FIU and are conditions for Egmont Group
membership. A rapid FIU-to-FIU exchange of financial intelligence across bor-
ders, which is enabled by the Egmont network, is faster than going through
other government information-sharing channels.

According to FATF Recommendation 40 and the related Interpretative Note,
countries should ensure that their competent authorities, including FIUs, provide the widest range of international cooperation in relation to money laundering, associated predicate offenses, and terrorist financing. The FATF also requires
that there should be a lawful basis for providing such cooperation and, among
other things, introduces specific obligations related to the exchange of information between FIUs. Similarly, the Egmont Group in its documents also advocates
for the widest possible cooperation between FIUs and sets up detailed principles
for information exchange between FIUs.[25]

As mentioned, the Egmont Group, the FATF, and other global standard setters do not regulate the FIU power to postpone suspicious transactions. In the
absence of precise international legal provisions, it could only be recommended
that similar principles and conditions related to the exchange of information
between the FIUs should also apply to international cooperation for postponing
suspicious transactions. Moreover, the FIU postponement power is a coercive
measure, and its international application clearly suggests introducing the necessary safeguards and calls for explicit regulation in both the requesting and
requested jurisdictions.

It is therefore recommended that jurisdictions consider enacting legislation
regulating all aspects of the international cooperation between the FIUs related
to the postponement power. Such cooperation might take into account the following principles:

- Same rules of confidentiality, protection of personal data, grounds for refusal
  to grant assistance, and conditions related to the use of information as those
  that apply under the Egmont Group and other international standards in
  respect of cooperation between FIUs could also apply for the international

postponement of transactions. Regarding the grounds for refusal to postpone a suspicious transaction, in addition to the above, the requested FIU may also refuse to provide assistance if such postponement could not be taken under its domestic law, had it been a similar domestic case.

- A request for postponement should contain all relevant factual and legal information, including a description of the case and information related to the funds, accounts, and transactions in a specific financial institution or DNFBP in the requested jurisdiction. A request should also contain other data necessary for satisfying the conditions related to the formal triggers for a postponement in the requested FIU, and information regarding the intended follow-up (a mutual legal assistance request for provisional measures) by the judicial or other competent authorities of the requesting jurisdiction.
- Postponing a transaction on behalf of a foreign FIU may be subject to the principle of reciprocity.
- Due to the expected urgency related to the international requests for postponement, the requested FIU should be able to act rapidly and give to such requests the same priority as in a similar domestic case.
- The requested and the requesting FIUs should be able to provide each other feedback in respect of follow-up decisions taken by the judicial or other competent authorities in both jurisdictions.
- At the operational level,[26] the FIUs should develop effective mechanisms for coordination of their activities related to international postponement of transactions, including a designation of readily available contact points and decision makers.

Operational Recommendations

Promote and facilitate the effective use by FIUs of their power to postpone suspicious transactions.

The survey data collected in this study show that of the FIUs that reported having this power, some 27 percent do not appear to use the power (have not used it during the three-year time frame of the collected data). Sixteen percent have used it, but only very infrequently—only one to three times over the same time period. These two groups are made up overwhelmingly of small FIUs, in small jurisdictions, and many of them are fairly new FIUs.[27]

Exercised judiciously, the power to postpone suspicious transactions can be a useful element of an FIU tool kit, and can be an important mechanism to prevent suspect funds from being removed from or fleeing the jurisdiction in which they have been detected and reported to the authorities. It seems likely that inexperience in the use of the power, and/or lack of awareness of the experience and capabilities of other FIUs, perhaps complicated by an absence of clear procedures and the nature of a posteriori reported suspicious transactions may be factors, among others, contributing to the infrequent use, or nonuse, of the power.

The Egmont Group, and donor agencies, may wish to consider closer inquiry into the reasons why many FIUs are not, or only infrequently, exercising this power, with a view to initiating programs to familiarize FIUs with the effective use of this power.

Develop and implement training of FIU and reporting entity staff on the procedures for use and application of the postponement power.

The majority of FIUs participating in the survey provide specific training to staff (66 percent of respondent FIUs) and to reporting entities (73 percent of respondent FIUs) on handling postponement cases, but less than half of respondent FIUs have a procedures manual for handling postponements.[28]

Decisions to use the power of postponement, and the conditions under which it could or would be used, are quite complex, and usually must be made in very tight time frames. Those decisions can involve a number of considerations, ranging from the factors or threshold indicators that might trigger a postponement action, to the extent of the application, the risk of alerting the client or suspect about the postponement, the risk of flight of funds or suspect(s), and the necessary coordination with law enforcement and prosecutorial authorities.

Because of these complexities, it is valuable for FIUs that expect to undertake postponement actions to:

- Develop and document standard procedures to assess incoming transaction information as to the possibility or requirement of postponing the transaction(s)
- Document the steps to be followed in processing such cases through the decision, and the implementation of the decision to postpone
- Designate FIU staff who may be involved in such processes, and provide training to such staff and decision makers as to the appropriate procedures and factors to be considered, as well as the advice, guidance, or direction that should be given to reporting entities and to competent investigative and prosecutorial authorities.

Reporting entities, whose task it is to assess proposed transactions of their clients, are required to report suspicious transactions to the FIU. Depending on local practice, reporting entities often find themselves in difficult and/or vulnerable situations when they need to alert the FIU to the probable need or desirability of postponing a transaction. To facilitate the effective interaction between the FIU and reporting entities in respect of possible postponements, it is recommended that the FIU:

- Issue guidance to reporting entities as to the form and manner of notification of a prospective postponement, the supporting information that should be included, and the expeditious delivery of notification to the FIU.

- Provide training to reporting entities on the factors and procedures involved in making a decision to postpone a transaction, and on the FIU's information requirements in reaching a decision. Clear understanding and awareness of each other's roles and responsibilities will facilitate taking a well-founded decision in the shortest time possible.
- Donor agencies, together with the Egmont Group, may wish to offer training and technical assistance to interested FIUs to build up their capacity to use this power. In particular, advice and training would be useful in the appropriate use of the power, the arrangements, and relationships that need to be put in place to act in a timely fashion, the triggers of any particular postponement, and the follow-on action that should flow from a postponement.

Develop and implement collection by the FIU of comprehensive operational statistics on the use of the power to postpone transactions and the follow-on actions that flow from those transactions.

The survey shows that only a small number of FIUs collect and keep meaningful statistical data on postponements and follow-on activities and final outcomes of their postponement orders.[29]

FIUs are required by the FATF standards to collect and retain statistical information about their operational activities for the purposes of review and to facilitate their assessment of the FIU's achievement of its operational objectives. Such data collection and analysis also makes possible the review of the effectiveness of various FIU processes and actions, and the allocation of resources to key functions. Although the collection of statistical information about postponement actions is not directly covered by FATF Recommendations, jurisdictions should consider including such data in their collection efforts. This can be especially useful in regard to this activity, which is difficult to plan for, arises very quickly, and can override other operational priorities, and may consume a lot of staff time in intense bursts of activity. In addition, such events are also likely to trigger urgent unplanned activity among the FIU's partners in law enforcement and prosecutorial agencies.

For these reasons, it is important for the FIU and other agencies involved in postponements of transactions to be able to periodically assess whether the results of the activity, in terms of follow-on interventions such as freezing of assets, criminal charges and prosecutions, convictions, and confiscations, justify the expenditures of the resources needed to conduct postponements of transactions and the follow-on interventions.

The collection of such data needs to be a multiagency undertaking[30] to ensure that all relevant information is collected and can be shared among the partner agencies. Since the FIU occupies a pivotal role near the front of any postponement process, it would be useful for the FIU to develop a data-gathering initiative in conjunction with its partners and to agree on processes and respective responsibilities for recording, gathering, and sharing these data.

Develop and implement effective mechanisms for coordination of the activities of reporting entities and public authorities involved in the postponement of transactions and follow-on interventions that may be triggered by postponement.

According to the survey, in less than half of the respondent jurisdictions (42 percent) are FIUs required to inform the judicial, prosecutorial, and law enforcement authorities about their postponement order, and there is an obvious lack of cooperation between the FIUs and other public authorities in these jurisdictions as regards the expected follow-on procedures.[31]

The postponement of a suspicious transaction is by its nature a short-term, interim measure. It is ordered by the FIU, but ultimately for the benefit of other competent authorities. Postponement of suspicious transactions is a multiparty endeavor, involving reporting entities, the FIU, law enforcement authorities, prosecutors and, ultimately, the courts. The process frequently begins with a suspicious transaction report from a reporting entity, sometimes accompanied by a request or recommendation to postpone the transaction. The FIU will need to interact with the reporting entity, and at the same time consult with the competent law enforcement authorities and/or prosecutor to ensure that those authorities will be willing and able to initiate more formal proceedings in respect of the transaction and/or the conductor or owner of the funds.

In the interest of avoiding the client or suspects learning about the postponement, these interactions and consultations must take place in a compressed time frame. It is therefore recommended that:

• All of the parties know their responsibilities
• There be designated and readily available contacts in the reporting entities and in the competent law enforcement authorities' and prosecutor's office
• Information necessary to guide their actions and decisions is readily available and easily transmitted to the appropriate recipients.

To this end, the FIU, together with other partners, would usefully establish documented processes and procedures for each partner's participation and agree in advance among themselves as to the appropriate contact points and decision makers. Although the FIU is situated near the front of that process, it can, at most, apply a short-term suspension of the transaction. It is law enforcement and prosecutorial authorities that must make a quick decision as to whether they will proceed with more formal measures to investigate and initiate judicial measures to freeze or seize the funds or assets in question.

Notes

1. See appendix B for examples of jurisdictional arrangements related to the FIU postponement power.
2. See appendix A, section "Legal Basis for the Power to Postpone a Suspicious Transaction at the Jurisdiction Level" for more detail.

3. See appendix A, section "Conditions for the Postponement of Suspicious Transaction" for more detail.

4. See appendix A, section "Conditions for the Postponement of Suspicious Transaction" for more detail.

5. Jurisdictions may provide for additional triggers that could be taken into account by FIUs; for example, a person is known to be the subject of an ongoing investigation of money laundering or financing of terrorism or a predicate offense; a person is the subject of an arrest warrant in a national or foreign jurisdiction; and so forth.

6. It is considered to be appropriate that jurisdictions apply the "reasonable grounds to suspect" as an objective test of suspicion that can be satisfied if the circumstances surrounding the transaction would lead a reasonable person to suspect that the transaction is related to a criminal activity. Subject to their legal systems, jurisdictions may apply a higher level of suspicion (for example, "serious grounds to suspect"), yet they should take into account that it might be impracticable for FIUs to reach a higher threshold in the limited time available to assess the use of the postponement power.

7. See appendix A, section "Application to Offenses" for more detail.

8. See appendix A, section "Application to Transactions" for more detail.

9. See FATF Recommendations 20 and 23.

10. For example, in some jurisdictions, casinos are allowed to pay out big jackpots to customers in several installments. In such cases, the FIUs can postpone the execution of payments if it suspects that the transactions are related to terrorist financing, money laundering, or underlying predicate offenses. Similarly, a lawyer or a notary who carries out a transaction for a client related to buying or selling of real estate or who is managing client's accounts or assets, should have sufficient time to report a related suspicious transaction, thus also giving sufficient time to FIU to postpone it. The same applies to real estate agents when they are involved in suspicious transactions for their client concerning the buying or selling of real estate.

11. According to FATF Recommendation 21, the "prohibition of tipping off" applies to reporting entities that should be "prohibited by law from disclosing the fact that a suspicious transaction report or related information is being reported to the FIU." The objective of this provision is to avoid suspect funds being transferred out of the reporting institution, and to avoid prejudicing investigations by making suspects aware of them; thus, it is similar to the objective of the FIU postponement power. In this report, the term "tipping off" will be used more broadly and will also include situations in which the countries' legislation prohibits the reporting entities from informing the client, suspect, or third persons that the postponement of transactions has been ordered.

12. See appendix A, section "Duration of the FIU Postponement Order" for more detail.

13. In the 2011 book, *Barriers to Asset Recovery* (see Stephenson et al. 2011, 102), the authors recommended that jurisdictions develop and implement policies and procedures to ensure that informal assistance channels are available to foreign practitioners for noncoercive measures and temporary freezes for 72 hours or less [authors' emphasis], without disproportionate or unduly restrictive conditions. This recommendation, although related to international cooperation in criminal matters, clearly advocates a similar postponing period, as is recognized as appropriate by most jurisdictions participating in the World Bank–Egmont Group survey.

14. A significant number of jurisdictions require reporting entities to refrain from carrying out a suspicious transaction until they have informed the FIU, and they also provide the maximum time period for such a delay. See appendix A under section "Conditions for the Postponement of Suspicious Transaction" for more detail.

15. See appendix A, section "Duration of the FIU Postponement Order" for more detail.

16. See appendix A, section "Liability for Damages" for more detail.

17. See appendix A, section "Application to Offenses" for more detail.

18. See, in particular, UNSC Resolution 1735 (2006).

19. This is only relevant for countries that ratified the convention.

20. See appendix A, section "Form and Content of the FIU Postponement Order" for more detail.

21. This recommendation applies only if both the requesting and the requested FIUs' countries have in place a regime for postponement of a transaction.

22. Of 22 jurisdictions that have ratified the Warsaw Convention, only three have made a reservation or declaration regarding the postponement of suspicious transactions on behalf of a foreign FIU.

23. See appendix A, section "Postponement on behalf of a Foreign FIU" for more detail. It is more likely that the FIU will postpone a transaction on behalf of a foreign FIU when, prior to receiving a request for postponement, the two FIUs are already engaged in an exchange of information regarding the suspect or transactions, so that the decision to postpone could be "foreseen" by both FIUs in the course of their interaction.

24. See FATF Recommendation 40.

25. See the Egmont Statement of Purpose and the Egmont Principles for Information Exchange between FIUs for Money Laundering Cases (http://www.egmontgroup.org/library/egmont-documents).

26. Where postponement is not feasible due to time restrictions or difficulties in obtaining relevant information, it is recommended that the FIUs consider "letting a transaction go through" for additional follow-up and monitoring in the foreign jurisdiction and keep the dialogue flowing for the possibility of a later postponement opportunity.

27. See appendix A, section "Aggregate Statistics" for more detail.

28. See appendix A, section "Operational Procedures" for more detail.

29. See appendix A, sections "Aggregate Statistics" and "Illustrative Examples" for more detail.

30. In addition to the FIU, the designated law enforcement and prosecutorial authorities and the competent judicial authorities should participate in the collection of data.

31. See appendix A, section "Obligation to Inform" for more detail.

Report with the Findings and Analysis

Methodology

Questionnaire

To carry out this study, a joint World Bank–Egmont Group project team was established in March 2011. A Concept Note and survey questionnaires were approved on May 11, 2011, by a team of peer reviewers representing both organizations. The questionnaire, consisting of 58 questions on various aspects of Financial Intelligence Units (FIUs') powers (and practices) to postpone suspicious transactions, was sent to 120 Egmont Group members and 14 selected non–Egmont Group FIUs on May 12, 2011.

During the first phase of the study (June 2011), the project team received responses from 74 FIUs and presented a preliminary report of the findings to the Egmont Legal Working Group during its meeting in Yerevan, Armenia, in July 2011. At that meeting it was agreed that the project team should reach out again to those FIUs that had not yet responded to the questionnaire but had indicated in their responses to the 2009 Egmont Biennial Census that they have the power to postpone suspicious transactions. The team conducted further outreach, and by the end of August 2011 had received responses from 88 FIUs.

During the second phase, in August-September 2011, the team followed up with those FIUs that had submitted incomplete responses and received additional responses from several, though not all, FIUs. In October 2011, the project team approached 13 selected FIUs to solicit some sanitized cases for inclusion in the study report, and received 16 sanitized cases from 11 jurisdictions related to their use of the postponement power. The collection of data and the description of findings were completed in December 2011.

Overview of Responses

The questionnaire was sent to 120 Egmont members and 14 selected non-Egmont members. Responses were received from 88 FIUs, of which 76 responses were from Egmont member FIUs (63 percent of Egmont members) and 12 were from non-Egmont members (86 percent of selected non-Egmont members).[1] The overall response rate was 67 percent and was higher than the 60 percent expected minimum response rate agreed by the World Bank and the Egmont Group.

Of the 88 respondent FIUs, 62 indicated that they have a power to postpone suspicious transactions. Fifty of those 62 respondents came from Egmont-member FIUs.

Existing Egmont information shows that 65 members have the power to postpone suspicious transactions. Thus, the 50 responses received in this study, from member FIUs with the power to postpone, represent 77 percent of all Egmont-member FIUs with the postponement power.

Of the respondent FIUs, 26 indicated that they do not have the power to postpone transactions, and only provided responses about their role in the postponement process carried out by other state bodies.

The respondent FIUs are representative of the overall population of FIUs on dimensions, such as type and size of FIU, and geographic representation (tables A.1–A.3).

Table A.1 FIU Responses by Type of FIU

Type of FIU	Number of FIUs with Postponement Power (%)	Number of FIUs without Postponement Power (%)
Administrative	39 (63)	16 (62)
Police	10 (16)	6 (23)
Hybrid	12 (19)	4 (15)
Prosecutorial	1 (2)	0

Source: World Bank data.
Note: FIUs = Financial Intelligence Units.

Table A.2 FIU Responses by Size of FIU

Size of FIU	Number of FIUs with Postponement Power (%)	Number of FIUs without Postponement Power (%)
Small (<50 staff)	50 (81)	16 (62)
Medium (50-100 staff)	8 (13)	5 (19)
Large (>100 staff)	4 (6)	5 (19)

Source: World Bank data.
Note: FIUs = Financial Intelligence Units.

Table A.3 Geographic Representation of the Respondent FIUs

Geographic Region	Number of FIUs with Postponement Power (%)	Number of FIUs without Postponement Power (%)
Europe	39 (63)	6 (23)
Africa/Middle East	8 (13)	0
Asia/Pacific/Oceania	8 (13)	8 (31)
Americas	7 (11)	12 (46)

Source: World Bank data.
Note: FIUs = Financial Intelligence Units.

Explanatory Note on Numbers of Responses

Although 88 FIUs responded to this survey, in many instances the numbers reported on a particular issue or question do not necessarily add up to 88. There are several reasons for this:

- Not all FIUs responded to every survey question.
- Some questions permitted more than one answer to be chosen.
- Sometimes, respondents marked several choices where only one was expected.
- In some cases, the first part of a question was answered, but no responses were given to subquestions, or vice versa.
- Sometimes respondents chose "Other" but did not explain what that meant.
- On some open-ended questions, many different responses were received, but only some of them were usable in the report.

Description and Findings

In this report, the analyzed responses to the questionnaire are focused on two main thematic headings: (a) the legal aspects of the FIU power to postpone suspicious transactions, and (b) the operational aspects of the FIU power to postpone a suspicious transaction. The report also presents selected statistics on the use of the postponement power provided by some of the respondents, and a number of sanitized cases received from the selected number of FIUs.

Legal Aspects of the FIU Power to Postpone Suspicious Transactions

Authority to Postpone Suspicious Transactions

In 26 respondent jurisdictions whose FIUs do not have the postponement power, 12 FIUs indicated that other bodies or state agencies have this power. The majority of FIUs (eight) in these jurisdictions are informed of postponement orders issued by other bodies or agencies and seven FIUs play some role in that postponement process. Their role is usually limited to proposing or recommending the postponement to the prosecutorial or judicial authorities. Three of these seven FIUs also responded that in the past three years they have been called upon to contribute to a postponement decision taken by another body and provided the requested statistical data.[2]

Of 26 respondent FIUs without the postponement power, 16 declared themselves as administrative-type FIUs, 6 as police-type FIUs, and 4 as hybrid-type FIUs.

Legal Basis for the Power to Postpone a Suspicious Transaction at the Jurisdiction Level

In this section we report on the legal systems of the 62 jurisdictions in which FIUs have the authority to postpone suspicious transactions, on the legal or statutory basis for such authority, and on cases where this FIU power has been challenged before the courts in regard to its legality or constitutionality.

The majority of FIUs (42, or 68 percent) are based in civil law jurisdictions, while a smaller number (16, or 26 percent) are found in common law jurisdictions. A small number of FIUs (4, or 6 percent) are found in jurisdictions that apply both legal systems. In 58 of 62 jurisdictions (94 percent), there is an explicit legal basis for the authority to suspend suspicious transactions, and in most instances (51 jurisdictions, or 82 percent) this authority is set out in the AML/CFT law or in the law creating the FIU (9 countries, or 15 percent).

Three of the four FIUs without an explicit legal basis for their power to suspend suspicious transactions are found in common law jurisdictions. Two of these FIUs are a police-type FIU and two a hybrid-type FIU.

The FIU power to postpone suspicious transactions has been challenged in eight jurisdictions. Five of them described the related circumstances in more detail and identified the following reasons that have been cited in suits brought against reporting entities or the FIU:

- Breach of the contractual duty of a bank to proceed with client's instructions
- The FIU power affected the constitutional rights of an individual (client)
- Breach of an individual's right to property
- Duration of the "informal freeze" was argued to be unreasonable after a significant period of time
- The client had proved the legal origin of money involved in the postponed transaction.

Court decisions in four jurisdictions were supportive of the use of the FIU power in the cases mentioned above, and in one jurisdiction this is still subject to a judicial review.

Application of the FIU Power to Postpone

FIUs were asked to provide information regarding several additional legal aspects of their power to suspend transactions, such as the applicability of this power to certain offenses and transactions, the conditions that need to be met in order to suspend a transaction, the right of appeal, the form of postponement order, and whether the postponement power is discretionary or mandatory. These aspects can potentially affect FIU's capacity to efficiently fulfill their mandates in regard to this power. They can also have an impact on the frequency of use of the power, and can define the degree to which an FIU can effectively manage the risks associated with its use.

Application to Offenses

Table A.4. lists the offenses in relation to which the 62 FIUs can apply their power to postpone suspicious transactions.

Examination of the narrative comments provided by respondents added some additional depth to the picture shown in table A.4.[3] With the exception

Table A.4 Application of the FIU Postponement Power to Offenses

Postponement Power Applicable to Criminal Offenses	Number of FIUs (%)	Postponement Power Applicable to Administrative Offenses/Misdemeanors	Number of FIUs (%)
Money laundering	53 (85)	Related to implementation of UNSC Resolutions	31 (50)
Financing of terrorism	52 (84)	Other	4 (6)
Predicate offenses for ML	33 (53)		
Any criminal offense	16 (26)		

Source: World Bank data.

Note: FIUs = Financial Intelligence Units; UNSC = United Nations Security Council; ML = money laundering.

of one FIU that can apply the postponement power only to financing of terrorism, all other FIUs can apply this power to both money laundering and terrorist financing. The number of FIUs that can also use this power in relation to predicate offenses for money laundering (53 percent) or any other offenses (26 percent) is still high, but it clearly shows that the main rationale for this power is to prevent the execution of transactions related to money laundering or terrorist financing.

The reported results regarding the use of the postponement power in relation to administrative offenses or misdemeanors raise some potential conflicts about the use of this power. Specifically, half of the responding FIUs indicated that they can also use the postponement power in relation to the implementation of the UNSC Resolutions related to terrorism.

Application to Transactions
A question that immediately arises when considering the power to postpone transactions is whether the power is applicable only to transactions that are reported as suspicious or can be applied more broadly once a suspicion is identified. Nearly one-quarter of the FIUs (14, or 23 percent) responded that they can only postpone transactions involving funds identified in the reporting entity's or state body's report or request. The remaining 48 FIUs (77 percent) are less constrained, and their power of postponement can also be extended to other funds or transactions, as shown in table A.5. In other words, these FIUs can freeze or block the account(s) of the suspect and not just his or her attempted transactions.

Similarly, nearly all of the respondent FIUs (57, or 92 percent) indicated that they can postpone transactions conducted at all reporting entities, and only a small number (5, or 8 percent) noted that they are limited to transactions carried out in financial institutions.

Conditions for the Postponement of Suspicious Transaction
This section examines whether the exercise of this power is mandatory or at the FIU's discretion. The majority of FIUs responded that they have full discretion regarding the use of this power (44, or 71 percent), while only 7 (11 percent)

Table A.5 Application of the FIU Postponement Power to Transactions

Postponement Power Applicable to Transactions	Number of FIUs (%)
Postponement of other or all transactions on the same account	43 (69)
Postponement of other financial transactions at the same reporting entity	34 (55)
Postponement of transactions in respect of deposited funds at other reporting entities	33 (53)
Other[a]	18 (29)

Source: World Bank data.
Note: FIUs = Financial Intelligence Units.
a. Those FIUs selecting "Other" mentioned, among other things, that they can extend the postponement power to "all assets—not limited to accounts"; "accounts linked to the account or holder of the account that is the subject of the STR"; "other persons and assets that could be linked with the original STR"; and the "FIU can freeze any account and not only individual transactions."

indicated that the use of this power is mandatory, provided certain conditions are met.

A number of FIUs (13, or 21 percent) responded that, depending on circumstances, the use of this power can be either mandatory or discretionary, and provided the following examples of determining circumstances in this regard:

- Mandatory when an STR sets out a suspicion of financing of terrorism and discretionary when there is a suspicion of ML
- Mandatory when implementing the UNSC sanctions list and discretionary when it depends on the requirements of an investigation
- Mandatory when the FIU has reasonable grounds to suspect that an offense of ML/FT could occur if a transaction proceeded
- Mandatory when based upon the request of the criminal judicial authority
- Mandatory for first 10 days and discretionary for the additional period of time
- Mandatory if there is strong indication of a certain crime.

With regard to the factors and/or conditions that can trigger the use of the FIU postponement power, a vast majority of FIUs (57, or 92 percent) indicated the STR notification as the prevailing factor, and more than half of FIUs (37 or 60 percent) cited their own analysis as the second-most-important factor. Requests from other bodies or entities were mentioned as "triggers" by a fewer, but still a significant number of, FIUs, as follows:

- Requests from law enforcement agencies: 29 FIUs (47 percent)
- Requests from reporting entities: 25 FIUs (40 percent)
- Requests by prosecutors: 21 FIUs (34 percent)
- Requests by other state bodies (for example, supervisory bodies and tax authorities): 7 FIUs (11 percent).[4]

The FIUs that have discretionary power to issue postponement orders identified several factors that they take into account in making their decisions. These factors are presented in table A.6.

Table A.6 Factors Influencing the FIU Discretionary Power to Postpone Transactions

Factors Taken into Account by FIUs	Number of FIUs (%)
FIU's own assessment of reasons to suspect ML/FT or predicate offenses	56 (90)
Reported suspicion of a reporting entity	49 (79)
Reason to suspect that the funds in question might leave the jurisdiction and be placed beyond reach	43 (69)
Reason to suspect that the conductor or owner of the funds might flee the jurisdiction	34 (55)
Specific request of a reporting entity	22 (35)
Whether a suspected transaction is domestic or international	17 (27)
Value of the transaction	11 (18)
Other routinely considered factors	5 (8)

Source: World Bank data.
Note: FIUs = Financial Intelligence Units; ML/FT = money laundering/financing of terrorism.

Table A.6 shows that in addition to making their own assessment of reasons of suspicion, more than half of the FIUs also take into account the reported suspicion of a reporting entity, and assess the risk that the funds or the owner might leave the jurisdiction.

In many jurisdictions, ascertaining the risk of "losing" funds suspected to be proceeds of crime is also one of the legal conditions that need to be met in order to issue a freezing or seizing order in the preinvestigative or investigative stage of a criminal procedure. The FIUs with postponement power might mitigate such a risk, and a significant number of FIUs consider this factor to be almost equally important to other legal or procedural factors.

Of the FIUs whose power to postpone suspicious transactions is either mandatory (7 FIUs) or both mandatory and discretionary depending on circumstances (13 FIUs), 11 responded that they might object to such mandatory applications if certain criteria are met. These criteria are shown in table A.7.

With regard to the level of suspicion needed for the FIU to activate its postponement power, almost all FIUs (56, or 90 percent) reported that they need to establish their own suspicion that a transaction is related to ML/FT. Several FIUs noted that they also take account of reporting entities' suspicion

Table A.7 Legal/Operational Grounds for FIU to Object to Mandatory Postponement

Grounds to Object	Number of FIUs (%)
Another body has already sought a postponement	3 (15)
The transaction has already been reviewed and the suspicion found to be unsubstantiated	7 (35)
The postponement of the transaction would carry a high risk of alerting the conductor of the transaction or owner of the account	5 (25)
It would be likely to compromise an ongoing investigation	6 (30)
Other grounds	3 (15)

Source: World Bank data.
Note: FIUs = Financial Intelligence Units.

(45 FIUs) and/or other state bodies' reported suspicion (26 FIUs) when making their decision, but only 6 FIUs (10 percent) mentioned the level of suspicion raised outside the FIU as the prevailing and mandatory factor in this context.

The survey also examined whether any legal provisions exist that empower (or constrain) reporting entities themselves to use the postponement power in relation to suspect transactions or accounts. In 45 jurisdictions (or 73 percent), the law provides an explicit obligation for reporting entities to refrain from carrying out a suspicious transaction until they have informed the FIU. This number is lower than one might expect, since the Third EU AML/CFT Directive contains an explicit obligation for member states in this regard.[5] Of these 45 FIUs, 42 explained that reporting entities themselves must delay the execution of a suspicious transaction for:

- 24 hours   6 FIUs
- 48 hours   7 FIUs
- 72 hours   5 FIUs
- Other[6]   24 FIUs.

Of the 60 respondent FIUs, nearly half (26, or 43 percent) noted that reporting entities are obliged to suspend reported suspicious transactions until they receive the FIU's response. An analysis of these responses shows that of these 26 FIUs:

- 12 FIUs must respond to reporting entities within 24–72 hours
- 6 FIUs must respond within 5–10 days
- In 2 jurisdictions the reporting entities must wait until consent is given by the FIU
- In 1 jurisdiction the reporting entities must wait until the end of possible delay of suspicious transaction mentioned in their report
- 1 FIU reported that there is no legal time frame
- 4 FIUs did not provide any explanation in this regard.

When asked whether a reporting entity's prior postponement or withholding of a suspicious transaction is a prerequisite for use of the FIU power to postpone such transaction, the majority of FIUs (50, or 83 percent) responded negatively. Interestingly, 1 of the remaining 10 FIUs that responded positively indicated that while it can continue the suspension of transactions previously suspended by the reporting entity, it can also postpone suspicious transactions regardless of any prior actions taken by the reporting entity.

Duration of the FIU Postponement Order
The survey posed questions about maximum permitted duration of the FIU postponement order and whether the duration period is fixed. The maximum duration periods for 62 FIUs are presented in table A.8.

Table A.8 Maximum Duration Period of FIU Postponement Orders

Duration Period	Number of FIUs (%)
Less than 24 hours	1 (2)
24 hours or 1 working day	1 (2)
48 hours or 2 working days	6 (10)
72 hours or 3 working days	15 (24)
120 hours or 5 working days	12 (19)
6 to 7 days/working days	3 (5)
10 to 12 days/working days	4 (6)
28 to 30 days/working days	3 (5)
3 months	3 (5)
6 months	2 (3)
Not regulated	8 (13)
Other (combinations)	4 (6)

Source: World Bank data.
Note: FIUs = Financial Intelligence Units.

Table A.8 shows that more than half of the FIUs (33, or 53 percent) are grouped around the postponement periods of two, three, and five days/working days, with three days being the prevailing threshold for around one-quarter of the FIUs.

A number of FIUs (8, or 13 percent) reported that their laws do not provide for any limits with regard to duration of an FIU postponement order. Examination of the narrative responses showed some extreme differences among the 8 FIUs in this group. While 2 FIUs indicated that the postponement period must be "reasonable" or "until the court order has been served," 1 FIU reported that a certain transaction was suspended for nine years and that this case has now been challenged in court. The above-mentioned 8 FIUs, and the 5 whose postponement orders can be issued for three and six months, all are either police-based or hybrid (police-prosecutorial) types of FIUs.

A duration period is fixed in 50 jurisdictions (81 percent). In the remaining 12 jurisdictions (19 percent), some FIUs mentioned the following basis for determining the duration period:

- Nature or seriousness of the case and the possibility for a freeze court order
- Duration is determined by FIU on a case-by-case basis
- The postponement order is for the purpose of court-ordered applications.

With regard to the starting point for the permitted duration of the postponement order, the majority of FIUs (50, or 81 percent) noted that this period starts when the reporting entity receives the FIU order, and 5 FIUs (8 percent) mentioned as the starting point the expiration of the suspension power of the reporting entities. Other FIUs (7, or 11 percent) mentioned several other starting times as follows:

- When the FIU receives the STR
- When the FIU confirms receipt of the notification from the reporting entity
- After the signature of the FIU order

- When the transaction is actually stopped
- On the day following the day of issuing of the postponement order
- When the customer requires a transaction to be carried out.

The study also examined whether the laws of the respondent jurisdictions permit the FIU to renew a postponement and, if so for how long; the number of permissible renewals; and under what conditions. Fifty eight FIUs responded to the first part of the question. While 39 FIUs (67 percent) mentioned that they cannot renew the postponement order, the remaining 19 (33 percent) indicated that they can renew postponements. The latter also provided detailed responses regarding the duration and number of renewals. Both are presented in table A.9.

For more than half of the above-mentioned FIUs (11), certain specific procedural or substantive conditions must be met in order to renew the postponement order. These include the following:

- The evidentiary material needed and anticipated application to the court for a freeze order
- More time needed to complete the analysis or investigation
- Decision is taken by the court on the basis of the FIU request and the court needs to be satisfied with the grounds of suspicion provided by the FIU
- Submission of the FIU case referral to law enforcement authorities
- Agreement of the general prosecutor's office
- Change of circumstance can trigger a new postponement order.

The FIU analysis of suspicious transactions often leads to abandoning the initial suspicion and closing the ML/FT case when it is still in the hands of FIU. Examination of the FIUs' responses reveals that of 59 respondent FIUs, 37 (63 percent) indicated that they can cancel their postponement orders before the expiry date. A smaller number (16) noted that certain specific criteria must be met to cancel a postponement, such as follows:

- The initial suspicion has not been confirmed
- The legal origin of assets has been proven

Table A.9 Duration and Number of Renewals of FIU Postponement Power

Duration of Renewal	Number of FIUs (%)	Number of Renewals	Number of FIUs (%)
From 2 to 15 days	10 (52)	1	7 (37)
30 days or more	2 (11)	3	1 (5)
Not specified in the law	4 (21)	Not limited	3 (16)
Depending on the court	2 (11)	Not specified in the law	8 (42)
Until receiving the court order	1 (5)		

Source: World Bank data.
Note: FIUs = Financial Intelligence Units.

- When the investigation into the person or transaction ceases
- A formal restraining order has been obtained by competent authorities
- The infeasibility of achieving an effective investigation.

The 22 respondent FIUs that did not indicate an ability to cancel a postponement order before its expiry date provided the following answers:

- 17 FIUs (29 percent) reported that their laws do not permit them to lift their postponement orders earlier.
- 3 FIUs (5 percent) marked "nonapplicable" in this regard.
- 2 FIUs (3 percent) mentioned that "the law does not explicitly allow or forbid that a postponement order may be cancelled."

Obligation to Inform

This segment of the survey looks at whether the FIU is obliged to inform other state bodies or authorities when it issues a postponement order and whether the relevant laws require the client to be informed of the postponement, or whether notification is prohibited, along with the prohibition of "tipping off" required under the international AML/CFT standards. Although the international standards[7] do not refer directly to the postponement orders, it is logical that the prohibition of tipping off is also relevant in the context of the FIU postponement orders, especially if they were issued on the basis of a received suspicious transaction report.

The survey shows that in fewer than half of the respondent jurisdictions (26, or 42 percent) FIUs are required to inform other state bodies about their postponement order, and most of those FIUs mentioned prosecutors (17 FIUs) and designated law enforcement authorities (11 FIUs) in this regard. A smaller number of FIUs are obliged to inform (also) the court (3 FIUs), the office for seizure and confiscation (1 FIU), the tax police (1 FIU), the higher banking commission (1 FIU), the office of the national anticorruption commission (1 FIU), and the board of the central bank (1 FIU).

When asked about the time frame for informing the above-mentioned bodies, the vast majority of FIUs responded that this should be done in a very short period of time,[8] while only a very few FIUs responded that this should be done in "2 days" (1 FIU) and "5 days" (2 FIUs).

There were 61 responses to the question related to the prohibition of tipping off, indicating that in 52 jurisdictions (85 percent) there is no obligation to inform the client of the postponement order. In the remaining 9 jurisdictions (15 percent), the client must be informed of the postponement order by:

- The FIU (five countries)
- The reporting entity (three countries)
- The law enforcement or investigating authority (one country).

Only 5 FIUs specified the time frame within which the client needs to be informed about the postponement order and indicated that this should be done: "immediately" (2 FIUs), "at once unless the court has decided that there shall be no notification" (1 FIU), "in 24 hours" (1 FIU), and "after 5 days" (1 FIU).

The last part of this section identifies steps that the reporting entities and FIUs take to avoid tipping off the client or suspect as to the STR and/or postponement orders. Not surprisingly, responses were received from the same 52 FIUs mentioned above, which leads to the conclusion that these countries also extend the prohibition of tipping off to cases that involve the issuing a postponement order. In addition, 20 FIUs (38 percent) indicated that certain steps must be taken to avoid the client or suspect learning about the postponement order. Only a few FIUs, in addition to referring to the tipping off provision in their laws, provided concrete examples of such steps. They are as follows:

- The FIU must initiate discussions with the reporting entity to ensure that their staff are aware of "tipping off" legislation.
- If the client asks why the transaction has not been executed, the reporting entity must contact the FIU and act in accordance with FIU direction.
- The FIU may give the reporting entity instructions on procedure regarding the clients involved in the suspected transaction.

It remains unclear how the reporting entities in jurisdictions where FIUs are empowered to postpone a suspicious transaction for a longer period of time (for example, for more than 72 hours) explain to their clients why a certain transaction has not been executed. This can obviously lead to situations where despite the existence of a formal, de jure prohibition of tipping off, the client de facto learns about the postponement order.

Right to Appeal

Generally speaking, the right to appeal the decisions of courts and other state authorities that affect citizens' rights, duties, or legal interest, or to use any other legal remedy to do so, is one of the fundamental human rights recognized by most countries worldwide. It is also a common legal practice in the criminal law area in many countries to limit or prohibit the right to appeal certain investigative measures and special investigative techniques, such as, for example, search warrants, seizure of documents or suspected proceeds or instrumentalities, and undercover operations. In this segment of the survey, the question posed is whether anyone, and if so who, according to national legislation, has a right of appeal an FIU order to postpone a suspicious transaction.

All 62 FIUs responded to this question, and 35 of them (56 percent) indicated that their laws do not provide for a right to appeal their postponement orders. The remaining 27 FIUs (44 percent) responded affirmatively and reported that the following persons have the right to appeal in their jurisdictions:

- Client or suspect   25 FIUs
- Reporting entity   7 FIUs
- Legitimate owner of funds subject to postponement   20 FIUs
- Other   3 FIUs.

In examining the narrative responses and comparing the responses of the 27 FIUs with their previous responses, one potentially contradictory issue emerged. Of 25 FIUs that recognize the client's right to appeal their postponement order, 10 FIUs reported that neither the client nor any other state body can be informed of the postponement. In addition, 11 FIUs noted that they only have to inform the state bodies, and no one is allowed to inform the client or suspect. It remains unclear, therefore, how and when the clients or suspects in these 21 countries can actually exercise their right of appeal, if they are entitled to appeal but are kept unaware of the postponement order. The illogicality of this issue is confirmed by analysis of FIU responses to the question related to the content of their postponement orders. In particular, only one FIU includes in its postponement order a notification that the client has a right to appeal.

Interestingly, the analysis of the responses shows almost no correlation between the duration of the FIU postponement order and the right to appeal. While approximately half of the 27 FIUs (14 FIUs) whose laws provide for a right to appeal belong to the group of FIUs that can postpone suspicious transactions for 10 or more days, most of the remaining 13 FIUs are in the group of FIUs with the power to postpone transactions from 3 to 5 days.

Form and Content of the FIU Postponement Order

In normal circumstances, all FIUs are expected to issue their postponement orders in written form, with a possible exception of those FIUs that are only empowered to give or withhold their permission for a suspicious transaction to be carried out. However, in urgent cases there is an obvious need for FIUs to act quickly to prevent suspicious transactions being completed, especially in cases in which the funds involved could be transferred beyond the reach of the competent authorities.

The survey examined whether in such urgent circumstances FIUs have the authority to issue an oral postponement order. All 62 FIUs responded to this question. Twenty-eight FIUs (45 percent) indicated that they can issue an oral postponement order, and 34 FIUs (55 percent) reported that they cannot.[9] FIUs that responded positively also noted that they must issue a written order within the following timelines:

- Immediately/as soon as possible   6 FIUs
- Less than 24 hours   10 FIUs

- 24 hours   4 FIUs
- 24–48 hours   1 FIU
- 3 days   1 FIU
- 5 days   1 FIU
- Not specified in the law   2 FIUs
- Not clear   3 FIUs.

As can be seen from the above, nearly three-quarters of the FIUs must follow up an oral postponement order with their written order within 24 hours.

FIUs were also asked to specify the content of their written postponement orders. Fifty-eight FIUs responded to this question and the results are provided in table A.10.

The reported results for this segment of the survey raise some interesting issues about the content of the report. Nearly 70 percent of responding FIUs include in their report the first five data elements mentioned in the table. The number of FIUs in this (and other) group(s) is even higher, if we take into account that an additional 9 FIUs, which in their responses only marked "other," explained that although the content of their postponement order is not regulated by law, it would normally include all data mentioned in the table. Only one-third of FIUs reported that an explanation of their reasons for suspicion has to be included in their postponement orders. As mentioned above, only one FIU also includes in its order a notification that the client or suspect has the right to appeal it.

Postponement on Behalf of a Foreign FIU
Regarding the possibility of issuing a postponement order on behalf of a foreign FIU, the results were as follows:

- 39 FIUs (63 percent) responded positively to this question.
- 22 FIUs (35 percent) indicated that they cannot.
- 1 FIU (2 percent) noted that this is not regulated in legislation.

Table A.10 Content of the Postponement Order

Content	Number of FIUs (%)
Name and address of reporting institution	41 (71)
Legal basis for postponement	40 (69)
Name and address of conductor or client	38 (66)
Account type and number	40 (69)
Account owner	39 (67)
Type of suspended transaction	23 (40)
Value of transaction	23 (40)
Name and address of recipient or beneficiary of transaction	6 (10)
Reasons for suspicion	19 (33)
Duration of postponement	35 (60)
Other	16 (28)

Source: World Bank data.
Note: FIUs = Financial Intelligence Units.

Not surprisingly, most of the FIUs that responded positively to this question are European (over three-quarters of all responding European FIUs). However, such FIUs were also identified on all other continents. Of 39 FIUs, about half (20 FIUs) indicated that the legal basis for issuing a postponement order on behalf of a foreign FIU is explicitly provided in the AML/CFT Law. The remaining 19 FIUs reported that this issue is not regulated in their legislation (or did not mention the legal basis at all), and one FIU referred to the relevant provisions of the Warsaw Convention.

The survey also sought information on the operational experience of such cooperation between FIUs. Of the 39 FIUs that have the authority to issue a postponement order on behalf of a foreign FIU, only 15 (38 percent) have actually done so during the last three years. Seven FIUs each issued one postponement order on behalf of a foreign FIU during those three years. Four FIUs account for 19 (56 percent) of those orders. In total, 34 postponement orders were issued on behalf of foreign FIUs in the last three years.

Regarding the question of whether the FIU can request a foreign FIU to postpone suspicious transactions, the 61 responses are as follows:

- 39 FIUs (64 percent) responded positively to this question.
- 21 FIUs (34 percent) responded that they cannot make such requests.
- 1 FIU (2 percent) noted that this is not regulated in legislation.

Examination of the narrative comments provided by respondents added some additional depth to this picture and revealed that not all FIUs that responded positively or negatively to the first question are the same as those responding in the same fashion to the second question. The analysis shows that 3 FIUs, which can issue postponement orders on behalf of a foreign FIU, are not allowed to send such request to a foreign FIU. Similarly, we also identified 4 FIUs that cannot issue a postponement order on behalf of a foreign FIU, yet they can request such assistance from their foreign counterparts.

With regard to the legal basis for such request, one-third of FIUs (12 FIUs) that responded positively to this question reported that this is explicitly regulated in their AML/CFT legislation, 2 FIUs mentioned memorandums of understanding, 1 FIU referred to the Warsaw Convention, and others explained that they can do it although their laws are silent in this regard.

Of 39 FIUs that have authority to request a foreign FIU to postpone a suspicious transaction on their behalf, 8 FIUs have actually done so in the last three years. In the aggregate, 50 requests for postponement were made to foreign FIUs during that period; of those, 38 (76 percent) emanated from a single FIU.

It is clear from the above that although 39 FIUs (63 percent) can request another FIU to issue a postponement order on their behalf or can respond to such a request from a foreign FIU, in practice, this authority is used by only a small number of FIUs, and 2 or 3 FIUs account for most of such requests.

Liability for Damages

This segment of the survey sought information about situations in which FIU postponement orders do not lead to a prosecution, but result in identifiable losses to the conductor of the transaction or the owner of funds involved. The questions asked were related to the existence of redress procedures and provisions that protect the FIU staff against potential liability for losses incurred.

Of 59 responding FIUs, less than half (25, or 42 percent) reported that provisions or mechanisms for compensation for damages exist in their jurisdictions. While 24 FIUs mentioned that civil litigation procedures apply in such cases, one FIU noted that this is regulated in their administrative procedure code. The compensation in seven respondent countries is payable by the state, or the relevant ministry, or the FIU.

In 46 countries (78 percent), FIU staff involved in the postponement decision are shielded from civil liability for any losses suffered by the subject of the postponement order. Explicit legal provisions for such immunity exist in 27 countries, while in 30 countries the immunity is provided under the general indemnity for public officials acting in good faith.[10]

Operational Aspects of the FIU Power to Postpone Suspicious Transactions

This section of the report examines a number of operational factors, conditions, and capabilities that can have a bearing on the exercise of this power. In particular, it looks at timeliness of information flows and access to supplementary information, analytic procedures and processes, decision-making processes, and follow-up to postponement orders.

Operational Capability

Decisions as to possible postponements of suspicious transactions are almost by definition sensitive and time sensitive. FIUs that have such powers need to be able to discharge their responsibilities in a timely and confidential manner. The survey questionnaire posed a number of questions about operational capability, the responses to which are reflected in tables A.11 and A.12 and the narrative below.

Timeliness of Reporting, Accessing, and Processing of Relevant Information
As can clearly be seen in table A.11, the great majority of the 62 FIUs with postponement powers have the benefit of processes for the timely receipt of information from reporting entities, and promptly enter that information into the FIU database and initiate searching and matching against the FIU's information holdings. Fewer FIUs enjoy online access to supplementary information from governmental sources, as shown in table A.12, and only a small proportion have direct access to account holder information at financial institutions.

Operational Procedures for Determining Whether to Postpone Transactions

As already noted, suspicious transaction reporting from reporting entities is quickly assessed as to the possibility of dissemination to law enforcement, and/or the possibility of postponement of the transaction(s). The information is promptly

Table A.11 Timely Receipt and Treatment of STRs Coming to the FIU

Treatment of STRs Coming to the FIU	Number of FIUs (%)
Secure Electronic Reporting Mechanism for Receiving STRs:	
• From financial institutions	47 (76)
• From other reporting entities	40 (67)
Initial Assessment of Incoming STRs:	
• For possible dissemination to law enforcement authorities	57 (92)
• For possible postponement of the transaction(s)	52 (87)
Standard Reporting Format	52 (87)
Prompt Entry into FIU Database	52 (87)
Prompt Searching/Matching against Database	53 (88)

Source: World Bank data.
Note: STR = Suspicious Transaction Report; FIUs = Financial Intelligence Units.

Table A.12 Access to Supplementary Information to Facilitate Analysis

Direct, Online Access by FIU to:	Number of FIUs (%)
Account holder information at financial institutions	7 (11)
Law enforcement databases	29 (47)
Tax information	18 (29)
Other governmental databases	34 (55)

Source: World Bank data.
Note: FIUs = Financial Intelligence Units.

entered and searched against FIU databases. An analysis is conducted to determine whether dissemination to law enforcement and/or issuing a postponement order are warranted. This process can involve a number of steps and processes aimed at forming a solid judgment as to the suspicion of money laundering or terrorism financing, leading to a decision to issue a postponement order. Several levels of FIU personnel may be involved in the process that leads to the decision to order postponement. Tables A.13, A.14, and A.15 provide some perspective on the process and procedures invoked, and who in the FIU is involved in the determination and who makes the decision to postpone a transaction.

Operational Procedures
A slim majority of FIUs (33 of 62) indicate that STRs that may call for postponement of transactions are handled like any other STR coming into the FIU. The remaining FIUs indicated that prospective postponement cases are handled differently and/or apply special procedures. Interestingly, only 13 FIUs (21 percent) reported that postponement cases are assigned to designated staff or units (table A.13), but in reporting on the process for reaching a determination that postponement should be ordered (table A.16, below) 46 FIUs (74 percent) reported that "designated analysts" are involved in the process of making a determination to postpone a transaction. Twenty-four FIUs (39 percent) reported (table A.13) that postponement cases are handled in the FIU according to special analytic procedures.

Table A.13 Operational Procedures for Prospective Postponement Cases

Cases that may Involve a Postponement order are Handled in the FIU:	Number of FIUs (%)
Like any other STR coming into the FIU	33 (53)
Assigned to special unit/designated staff	13 (21)
In accordance with special analytic procedures	24 (39)
Information is stored in a special registry	13 (21)

Source: World Bank data.
Note: STR = Suspicious Transaction Report; FIUs = Financial Intelligence Units.

In terms of training and support for FIU staff involved in postponement cases, 41 FIUs (66 percent) reported that they provide specific training to staff on handling postponement cases, but only 27 (44 percent) reported that their FIU has a procedures manual for handling and approving postponements.

Reporting entities play a crucial role in initiating and implementing postponements, and it is normally their initial judgment as to suspicion that puts in train processes in the FIU that may result in decisions to postpone transactions. In particular, the quality and detail of the reported suspicion described in the STR will be one of the most significant factors to activate the FIU's consideration of a postponement.

FIUs appear to be conscious of this, and 45 FIUs (73 percent) indicated that they provide training to reporting entities' compliance staff on the procedures for postponement of suspicious transactions.

As can be seen in tables A.14 and A.15, an overwhelming majority of FIUs conduct a range of checks and searches, for the purpose of corroborating the suspicion of money laundering reported by a reporting entity. To a lesser extent, they also carry out such searches for the purpose of assessing the risk of flight

Table A.14 FIU Steps in Considering Postponement

The Following Steps are Commonplace:	Number of FIUs (%)
Search FIU database	61 (98)
Search law enforcement authority database	54 (87)
Check for accounts at other institutions	44 (71)
Check information at other state agencies	51 (82)
Check public and commercially available information	54 (87)

Source: World Bank data.
Note: FIUs = Financial Intelligence Units.

Table A.15 Objectives of FIU Searches and Analysis

Analysis is Conducted by FIU to Assess or Corroborate:	Number of FIUs (%)
Suspicion of the reported transaction	58 (94)
Risk of flight of the funds in question	46 (74)
Risk of flight of the suspect or account holder	34 (55)

Source: World Bank data.
Note: FIUs = Financial Intelligence Units.

of funds or flight of the suspect (which can often be inferred from the nature of the suspect transaction). While virtually all FIUs conduct processes to corroborate the suspicions reported by reporting entities in their STRs, only three-fourths of them indicate that they specifically conduct searches and analyses to assess or corroborate the risk of flight of funds. Only just over one-half also assess the risk of flight of the suspect or account holder.

These searches appear to be undertaken irrespective of whether the FIU in question has, or does not have, direct access to relevant information sources (see table A.12, above). For example, 44 FIUs indicate that they check for accounts at other institutions, but only 11 have direct access to such information. And 54 FIUs indicate that they search law enforcement authority databases, but only 29 have direct access to them. It seems probable, therefore, that for a substantial proportion of FIUs (that do not have ready, online access to the information sources) the completion of these checks and the determination of whether a postponement should be ordered is likely to be a time-consuming and resource-intensive process, likely spanning several days, rather than hours.

Decision-Making Processes

The preceding section examines the operational steps and processes involved in considering the postponement of a transaction. This section examines the question of who, at the FIU, is involved in preparing for the determination to postpone a transaction, and who, in particular, makes the decision to issue a postponement order. Table A.16 shows that a number of FIU staff members can be involved in the determination process. In some FIUs, even staff of other bodies (police, prosecutors) working in the FIU may be involved in this process.

Table A.17 suggests that in just over three-quarters of FIUs, the decision to postpone a suspicious transaction it taken by the head of the FIU. The actual proportion is somewhat higher, as the "Others" category, on examination of individual responses, includes primarily senior members of the FIU (including, in some cases, the head of analysis), who are authorized in one way or another to act on behalf of the head of the FIU in the latter's absence or unavailability.

Table A.16 Reaching a Determination to Postpone a Transaction

Actors in the FIU Involved in the Determination Process	Number of FIUs (%)
Designated FIU analyst	46 (74)
Head of analysis	35 (56)
FIU legal department	16 (26)
Head of the FIU	43 (69)
Others[a]	24 (39)

Source: World Bank data.
Note: FIUs = Financial Intelligence Units.
a. This includes other members of the FIU, prosecutors or police officers in the FIU, and the FIU board.

Table A.17 Making the Decision to Postpone a Transaction

FIU Postponement Decisions are made by:	Number of FIUs (%)
Head of the FIU	48 (78)
Head of analysis	6 (10)
Legal advisor of FIU	1 (2)
Designated analyst	1 (2)
Others[a]	25 (40)
External oversight or review of FIU decision	**10 (16)**

Source: World Bank data.

Note: FIUs = Financial Intelligence Units.

a. This category includes a variety of senior personnel who stand in for the head of the FIU in his or her absence, or specially designated deputies of the head, and the FIU board or commission, or a prosecutor.

In practice, therefore, in over 90 percent of FIUs the postponement decision is made by the appointed or designated "acting" head of the FIU. In a small number of cases, the FIU board or commission takes the decision, and in one case it is a prosecutor.

Only 10 FIUs (16 percent) report that the decision to postpone a transaction is subject to external oversight or review.

Postponement and Follow-up

Once the postponement decision has been made, the FIU delivers the order to the appropriate recipient. Of the 62 FIUs that responded, 59 (95 percent) indicated that the order is delivered to the reporting entity at which the transaction was initiated and which sent the STR to the FIU. Some FIUs also deliver the order to various other state agencies. Thirteen FIUs (21 percent) provide the order to the public prosecutor, 9 (15 percent) deliver it to a designated law enforcement agency, 3 FIUs (5 percent) deliver it to a court or competent judge, and 8 (13 percent) provide it to "other" recipients. The "other" category includes law enforcement officials. Presumably, when a postponement order has been issued, that fact is also contained in any financial intelligence dissemination to the relevant law enforcement authority.

One FIU is required to notify the client or suspect of the postponement order. After a postponement order is issued, 17 FIUs (27 percent) indicated, there is a requirement for the FIU to follow up with the law enforcement authority/prosecutor, or court before the expiry of the order.

Within the FIU, a decision to postpone a transaction is also accompanied by certain actions, as can be seen from table A.18. It is noteworthy that only two-fifths of the FIUs (25, or 41 percent) reported that they have procedures in place to follow up on postponement orders to ascertain what further action has flowed from the postponement.

In looking at the statistical data provided by FIUs on follow-on actions in their jurisdictions, it appears that in general only about 20 FIUs provided any statistical information about investigative and prosecutorial outcomes for 2008–10.

Table A.18 FIU Actions Following a Postponement Order

FIU Actions	Number of FIUs (%)
Close monitoring of the case	40 (65)
Accelerated analysis and dissemination to law enforcement authorities	45 (73)
More intensive analysis of the case	46 (74)
Special arrangements to prevent "tipping off"	17 (27)
A report on disposition at end of postponement	13 (21)
FIU Follow-Up on Postponement Orders to Ascertain:	
Whether law enforcement authorities conduct an investigation	26 (42)
Whether the prosecutor extends freeze of assets	25 (40)
The outcome of any investigation or prosecution	24 (39)

Source: World Bank data.
Note: FIUs = Financial Intelligence Units.

Table A.18 shows that only 17 FIUs (27 percent) apply special arrangements to prevent "tipping off," and only 13 FIUs (21 percent) make a report on the disposition of the case at the end of the postponement period.

Statistics

The survey questionnaire for this study asked respondents to provide selected statistics on the number of STRs received by the FIU, the number of postponements of transactions ordered, and actions following the postponement (for example, investigation, prosecution, conviction, and confiscation) for 2008–10. There are some limitations to the comparison and aggregation of the data, since some FIUs did not (or could not) provide data for all three years. Of the 62 participating FIUs with the power to postpone transactions, 6 FIUs provided no data at all in the statistics section of the questionnaire.

Aggregate Statistics[11]

Table A.19 shows the aggregate number of STRs received by the reporting FIUs, and the aggregate number of postponement orders issued by FIUs for 2008–10.

In 2010, a mere 6 FIUs accounted for 881 postponements, amounting to 62 percent of all reported postponements for that year. Three of those 6 FIUs provided no data on follow-on actions and three provided only partial data. For the same year (2010), 5 "outlier" FIUs reported receiving 87 percent

Table A.19 Aggregate Numbers of STRs Received and Postponement Orders Issued, 2008–10

Year	Number of STRs	Number of Postponement Orders	Number of FIUs Issuing Postponement Orders
2008	1,984,695	1,281	34
2009	2,248,070	1,224	42
2010	2,578,771	1,412	43

Source: World Bank data.
Note: STR = Suspicious Transaction Report; FIUs = Financial Intelligence Units.

of the total STRs reported by the 56 FIUs that provided STR data. Those same 5 FIUs accounted for only 24 percent of the total reported postponements. Three of those FIUs provided no data about dispositions. Of the remaining 2 FIUs:

- One received 16,000 STRs and issued 112 postponement orders, which led to 96 investigations, 35 convictions, and 13 confiscations
- The other FIU received 14,000 STRs and issued 201 postponements, which led to 38 investigations, 2 prosecutions, 5 persons convicted, and 8 confiscations.

Illustrative Examples

Since a significant number of FIUs did not or could not provide data on follow-on actions, it is not possible to make meaningful aggregate comparisons of postponements to investigations, prosecutions, convictions, and confiscations. As shown in table A.18, only about 40 percent of FIUs indicate that they follow up postponement orders to ascertain whether any investigations or prosecutions have occurred following postponement orders.

Tables A.20–A.23 present several illustrative examples for which all or most of the relevant information was provided by respondent FIUs, making possible the presentation of the data in the chain beginning with STRs received by the FIU through convictions and confiscations.

Table A.20 Results, Example 1

An FIU Received 360,000 STRs in One Year	Number of Actions Taken and Dollar Amount Confiscated (in US$)
• Postponement orders issued	75
• Longer freezes sought by prosecutor	52
• Ensuing investigations	35
• Prosecutions	6
• Convictions	1
• Confiscations	1 (US$123,000)

Source: World Bank data.
Note: FIU = Financial Intelligence Unit; STR = Suspicious Transaction Report.

Table A.21 Results, Example 2

A Small FIU Received 221 STRs in 2010	Number of Actions Taken and Dollar Amount Confiscated (in US$)
• Postponement orders issued	19
• Related accounts identified	10
• Investigations	19
• Prosecutions	4
• Convictions	1
• Confiscations	1 (US$26,000)

Source: World Bank data.
Note: FIU = Financial Intelligence Unit; STR = Suspicious Transaction Report.

Table A.22 Results, Example 3

An FIU Received 19,000 STRs in 2010	Number of Actions Taken
• Postponement orders issued	60
• Related accounts identified	25
• Investigations	25
• Prosecutions[a]	2

Source: World Bank data.
Note: FIU = Financial Intelligence Unit; STR = Suspicious Transaction Report.
a. No information was provided on convictions or confiscations.

Table A.23 Results, Example 4

A Small FIU Received 309 STRs in 2009	Number (In US$)
• Postponement orders issued	2
• Related accounts identified	2
• Longer freeze sought	2
• Investigations	1
• Prosecutions	1

Source: World Bank data.
Note: FIU = Financial Intelligence Unit; STR = Suspicious Transaction Report.

Notes

1. During the Egmont plenary meeting in July 2011, the Egmont membership was extended from 120 to 127 member FIUs. In addition, 5 FIUs (Azerbaijan, Kazakhstan, Mali, Morocco, and Uzbekistan), which had been on the list of 14 selected non-Egmont members, became members in July 2011.

2. All statistical data are presented below in subsection "Aggregate Statistics" on statistics.

3. While some respondents indicated more than one choice, others indicated only one.

4. A request from foreign FIUs or other competent authorities for postponing suspicious transactions on their behalf will be presented separately in section "Postponement on behalf of a Foreign FIU" of appendix A.

5. See chapter 2, section "International/Regional Standards" of the report. According to the FIUs' responses, out of 27 EU member countries, 22 are acting in accordance with article 24 of the Third EU AML/CFT Directive.

6. Those FIUs selecting "Other" mentioned the following additional time frames in this regard: "end of a time limit needed for a normal execution of the transaction," "end of the next working day," "until the FIU grants approval/takes a decision," "5 days," and "7 days."

7. See more in note 11 on page 35.

8. In their replies, the FIUs used the following wording in this context: "immediately," "without delay," "in few hours," or "within the duration of postponement."

9. One FIU explained that the postponement is effected either by the FIU withholding consent to a reported suspicious transaction or under the "freezing regime," and the oral postponing order is only applicable for the consent regime.

10. Eleven FIUs responded that they have both and that the general immunity provisions are also supplemented by the specific provisions.

11. While a large proportion of respondent FIUs provided statistics about STRs received and postponements issued, relatively few provided statistics about follow-on actions by law enforcement, prosecutors, or the courts.

Examples of Country Regulation Related to the FIU Postponement Power

This appendix presents examples of the various ways different countries regulate the use of the postponement power.

Country A

An example of an FIU with the following:

- An explicit legal basis to postpone transactions
- A short postponement period
- Procedures to mitigate tipping off.

Country A's FIU is small, with less than 50 staff members. It is an administrative-type FIU operating within a civil law legal system. There is an explicit legal basis giving authority to the FIU to postpone suspicious transactions within its AML/CFT law. The said law does not provide a right of appeal of the FIU's order to postpone a suspicious transaction.

The conditions that can trigger the use of the FIU power to postpone are an STR notification from a reporting entity along with the FIU's own analysis reaching a certain threshold; and cases opened on the basis of a written and reasoned initiative from the court, the prosecutor's office, local law enforcement agencies, the Intelligence and Security Agency, or the Customs Administration.

There is no legal requirement for a reporting entity to suspend all reported transactions until the FIU responds to the filing. However, a reporting entity is required to furnish the FIU with the data on the suspicious transaction prior to effecting the transaction and shall state the time limit within which the transaction is to be carried out. Such report may also be submitted by telephone (and the written report follows the next working day at the latest). In the case of such prior suspicious transaction reporting, a reporting entity waits for the FIU's feedback (in practice, that usually means several hours).

The following actions are taken by the FIU leading up to the decision to issue a postponement order in respect of a transaction:

- Search FIU transaction databases and disclosure database
- Search of law enforcement databases
- Check for accounts at other reporting entities
- Check information held by other agencies
- Check publicly or commercially available information
- Analysis is conducted to corroborate:
  - Suspicion of the reported transaction
  - Assumed risk of flight of the funds in question.

The FIU can postpone a suspicious transaction for 72 hours, which commences when the reporting entity receives the FIU's postponement order. There is no power to renew a postponement order. When the FIU issues a postponement order, it is obliged to inform the police and the State Prosecutor's Office. While there is no prescribed time frame for this notification, in practice the FIU informs the police and the State Prosecutor's Office at once. These authorities are obliged to act promptly so that they can take whatever action they deem appropriate within their competencies within the 72-hour period.

Following the issuance of a postponement order, there is no legal requirement for the client or suspect to be informed of the postponement. The FIU is actively involved in working with the reporting entity to avoid "tipping off" the client or suspect. The FIU identifies a liaison officer (and deputy) within the reporting entity, who will be the primary contact person for the FIU. Prior to issuing the postponement order, the FIU will check that the liaison officer, or his or her deputy, is on duty to receive the said order. By following such a procedure the FIU is able to reduce the number of employees within the reporting entity that have access to the confidential information or knowledge of the postponement.

Following the issuance of a postponement order, there may be the need to gather additional information during precriminal or criminal proceedings, or due to other justified reasons, the FIU may give the reporting entity instructions on procedure regarding the clients concerned in the transaction.

Country B

An example of an FIU with the following:

- **An explicit legal basis to postpone transactions**
- **A short yet renewable postponement period**
- **Domestic cooperation.**

Country B's FIU is a large FIU with more than 100 staff members. It is an administrative-type FIU operating within a civil law legal system. There is an explicit legal basis giving authority to the FIU to postpone suspicious transactions within its AML/CFT law and the enabling legislation for the FIU. The said law also provides a right of appeal of the FIU's order to postpone a suspicious transaction. This right is afforded to the client or suspect, the reporting entity, and the legitimate owner of the funds that are subject to postponement.

The reporting entity can postpone the transaction for two working days; this term may be extended by the FIU for five more working days. The FIU may also issue its own postponement order for five working days.

When the FIU issues the postponement order (or extends the reporting entity order), it immediately informs law enforcement agencies and the prosecutor's office. If the FIU finds enough facts to support a money-laundering or terrorist-financing suspicion, then it forwards the case to law enforcement and automatically extends the postponement for seven more working days. If the FIU drops the suspicions, it immediately informs the reporting entity.

Timely exchange of information is crucial in the case of postponement. To ensure that the FIU has all the necessary information it requires to determine whether it is necessary to issue a postponement order, case officers within the FIU immediately contact the relevant compliance officer within the reporting entity by phone to check for more details.

In all cases involving money-laundering or terrorist-financing suspicions, the FIU case officers contact law enforcement to ascertain whether they will conduct operational activities and if there was still a need to prevent the client from learning of the postponement order. Based on the law enforcement feedback, case officers will then contact the reporting entity's compliance officers and explain the situation.[1]

Country C

An example of an FIU with the following:

- An explicit legal basis to postpone transactions
- A short postponement period
- Follow-up procedures with law enforcement
- Domestic cooperation
- Procedures to mitigate tipping off.

Country C's FIU is medium size with between 50 and 100 staff members. It is an administrative-type FIU operating within a civil law legal system. There is an explicit legal basis giving authority to the FIU to postpone suspicious transactions within its AML/CFT law. The said law does not provide a right of appeal of the FIU's order to postpone a suspicious transaction.

The conditions that can trigger the use of the FIU power to postpone are an STR notification from a reporting entity, an STR notification by the federal prosecutor in terrorism-financing-related investigations, and foreign FIU requests.

In accordance with the AML/CFT law, the FIU can oppose execution of any transaction if it deems such action necessary due to the seriousness or urgency of the matter.

There is no legal requirement for a reporting entity to suspend all reported transactions until the FIU responds. However, a reporting entity is required to furnish the FIU with the data on a suspicious transaction prior to effecting the transaction. Reporting entities must suspend the disclosed transaction until the end of the delay they mentioned in the disclosure. Reporting entities are free to execute the transaction at the end of the mentioned delay unless the FIU issues a postponement order.

The, FIU can postpone a suspicious transaction for 48 hours, which will commence when the reporting entity receives the FIU's postponement order. There is no power to renew a postponement order. In general, when an FIU postponement order is issued, the case is sent to the prosecutor.

When the FIU issues a written postponement order (either by fax or by e-mail), it will immediately inform the reporting entity of this postponement order by phone. The reporting entity is also reminded of the AML/CFT law stipulating they may not, under any circumstances, disclose to the customer concerned or to third persons the fact that information has been transmitted to the FIU or that a money-laundering or terrorist-financing investigation is being or may be carried out.

When the FIU reports a file to the judicial authorities, these authorities are required to inform the FIU of all final decisions issued in these cases. In urgent cases or cases where assets of significant value can be seized, the head of analysis will contact the public prosecutor by phone and a liaison officer (that is seconded from the federal police and works within the FIU) will contact the competent police authorities.

Following a recent amendment of the AML/CFT law, the power to postpone a suspicious transaction has been extended to a maximum of five working days. The tipping off prohibition applies only to the first two working days of this period and no longer applies during the remaining working days of this period. Despite this legislative change, the FIU intends to maintain its current procedure and carry out all the necessary analysis within two days following the postponement order.

The AML/CFT law was also amended, formalizing the cooperation between the FIU and the Country C's central seizure or confiscation office. The FIU always informs this office when a postponement order is issued, or when assets of significant value, of any kind, are available for possible judicial seizure.

Country D

An example of an FIU with the following:

- An explicit legal basis to postpone transactions
- A short postponement period

- Follow-up procedures with law enforcement
- Domestic cooperation.

Country D's FIU is small with less than 50 staff members. It is an administrative-type FIU operating within a common law legal system. There is an explicit legal basis giving authority to the FIU to postpone suspicious transactions within its FIU law. The said law does not provide a right of appeal of the FIU's order to postpone a suspicious transaction.

The conditions that can trigger the use of the FIU power to postpone are an STR notification from a reporting entity, a specific request or recommendation from a reporting entity, the FIU's own analysis reaches a certain threshold, and a request from a law enforcement agency.

There is no legal requirement for a reporting entity to suspend all reported transactions until the FIU responds to the filing. However, the reporting entity would be required to suspend a suspicious transaction once it knows, suspects, or has reasonable grounds to suspect that the transaction or proposed transaction involves proceeds of criminal conduct and that the said funds may be immediately removed from the account or jurisdiction. A report is then made to the FIU.

The following actions are taken by the FIU leading up to the decision to issue a postponement order in respect of a transaction:

- A search of FIU transaction databases and disclosure databases
- A search of law enforcement databases
- A check for accounts at other reporting entities
- A check of information held by other state agencies
- A check of publicly or commercially available information
- Analysis is conducted to corroborate:
  - Suspicion of the reported transaction
  - Assumed risk of flight of the funds in question.

The FIU can postpone a suspicious transaction for 72 hours, which will commence when the reporting entity receives the FIU's postponement order.

The FIU maintains an excellent rapport with reporting entities, which allows for these institutions to immediately advise the FIU of a client that is highly suspicious and if not immediately acted upon may result in the assets being removed from the jurisdiction.

All STRs are immediately reviewed. The legislation governing the FIU gives it the power to request any additional information that is considered relevant to enable it to carry out it functions. Throughout this analytical process, the FIU is in constant dialogue with the reporting entity. This open communication channel allows the FIU to, if necessary, instantaneously exercise its authority if the circumstances warrant. Once the reporting entity's suspicion is confirmed, the director, under the FIU governing legislation, orders in writing any person to refrain from completing any transaction for a period not exceeding 72 hours.

The analytical report of the FIU and supporting documentation is immediately provided to law enforcement for investigation. The FIU maintains a close relationship with law enforcement and acts as the go-between for the reporting entity and law enforcement.

The FIU is empowered to freeze a bank account under suspicion for an additional five days upon request of the Commissioner of Police. This will in essence provide law enforcement with eight days to advance their investigation and seek additional restraint of the suspicious account. The reporting entity is advised in writing of the additional five-day freeze and is not able to deal with the account until the order to freeze expires without a restraining order issued by law enforcement or the aggrieved person successfully applies to a judge to discharge the FIU's order.

Country E

An example of an FIU with the following:

- **An explicit legal basis to postpone transactions**
- **A long postponement period**
- **Follow-up procedures with law enforcement**
- **Domestic cooperation.**

Country E's FIU is medium size with between 50 and 100 staff members. It is a police-type FIU operating within a common law legal system. There is an explicit legal basis giving authority to the FIU to postpone suspicious transactions within its AML/CFT law. The said law does not provide a right of appeal of the FIU's order to postpone a suspicious transaction.

To avoid being charged with committing the money-laundering offenses in the AML/CFT law, the reporting entity has to make an authorized disclosure[2] and obtain the appropriate consent[3] from the FIU. A key element of consent is the specification of time limits within which the authorities must respond to an authorized disclosure in circumstances where a consent decision is required. The law specifies that consent decisions must be made within seven working days.

The seven-day notice period commences on the day after a disclosure is made. The notice period consists of seven working days and excludes bank holidays and weekends. The purpose of the seven-day notice period is to allow the FIU and its law enforcement partners time to assess risk; and to analyze, research, and undertake further enquiries relating to the disclosed information in order to determine the best response to the request for consent. If nothing is heard within that time, then the discloser can go ahead with an otherwise prohibited act without an offense being committed.

A consent decision will usually be communicated to the reporting entity by telephone to provide the quickest possible response. The FIU will also send a letter by post recording the decision, but there is no requirement to wait for this letter in order to proceed with the prohibited act if consent has been granted verbally.

When consent is granted by the FIU, the reporting entity is free to undertake the reported prohibited act(s) without committing a money-laundering offense in relation to the act(s). Consent does not extend to any acts or criminal property not detailed in the initial disclosure or agreed with the FIU.

Where the FIU gives notice that consent to an act is refused, a further 31-day period (the "moratorium") commences on the day that notice is given. The 31 days include Saturdays, Sundays, and public holidays. It is an offense to undertake the act during this period since the participant would not have the appropriate consent. The moratorium period enables the FIU to further its investigation into the reported matter using the powers within the AML/CFT law in relation to the criminal property (for example, imposing a restraining order). If the moratorium period expires and no such action has been taken, the reporting entity is free to proceed with the act(s) detailed in the initial disclosure.

When seeking consent, the reporting entity should identify as clearly as possible:

- The suspected benefit from criminal conduct (the "criminal property"), including where possible the amount of benefit
- The reason(s) for suspecting that property is criminal property
- The proposed prohibited act(s) the reporter seeks to undertake involving the criminal property
- The other party or parties involved in dealing with the criminal property including their dates of birth and addresses where appropriate.

All requests for appropriate consent are treated as a priority within the FIU. The aim is to provide the quickest possible response to a reporter. As soon as a decision has been made in relation to a request for consent, it will be relayed to the reporter without delay.

Country F

An example of an FIU with the following:

- An explicit legal basis to postpone transactions
- A long and renewable postponement period
- Follow-up procedures with the prosecutor's office.

Country F's FIU is small with less than 50 staff members. It is a police-type FIU operating within a civil legal system. There is an explicit legal basis giving authority to the FIU to postpone suspicious transactions within its AML/CFT law. The said law does not provide a right of appeal of the FIU's order to postpone a suspicious transaction; however, the general provisions for appeal are stipulated in the Act of Administrative Procedures.

The conditions that can trigger the use of the FIU power to postpone are an STR notification from a reporting entity along with the FIU's own analysis, and notification from a law enforcement authority or prosecutor and a request from a foreign FIU.

There is no legal requirement for a reporting entity to suspend all reported transactions until the FIU responds to the filing. However, according to the AML/CFT law, an obligated person has the right to refuse concluding a transaction if a person or customer participating in the transaction or the official act, regardless of a respective request:

- Does not submit the documents or relevant information required for the customer due diligence measures or data and documents certifying the legal origin of the property constituting the object of the transaction; or
- If, on the basis of the data and documents submitted, the obligated person suspects that it may be money laundering or terrorist financing.

In that case, the obligated person will electronically submit an STR to the FIU with the notification "URGENT" (usually duplicated by telephone), and the FIU will undertake the analysis and take a decision regarding the postponement of the transaction within a few hours or the next working day.

The following actions are taken by the FIU leading up to the decision to issue a postponement order in respect of a transaction:

- A search of FIU transaction databases and the disclosure database
- A search of law enforcement databases
- A check for accounts at other reporting entities
- A check of information held by other state agencies (the tax authority, and so forth)
- A check of publicly or commercially available information (the business registry, and so forth)
- Analysis is conducted to corroborate:
  - Suspicion of the reported transaction
  - The assumed risk of flight of the funds in question.

In the event of suspicion of money laundering or terrorist financing, the FIU may issue a precept suspending a transaction or imposing restrictions on the disposal of an account or other property constituting the object of the transaction for up to 30 days as of the delivery of the precept. In the case of property registered in the land registry, ship registry, traffic registry, or commercial registry, the FIU may, in the event of justified suspicion, restrict the disposal of the property for the purpose of ensuring its preservation for up to 30 days. The postponement order (prescription) is an administrative act, which can be appealed, and therefore also the holder of the money or property will receive the copy of the prescription.

In practice, during the first 30 days there exists the reverse burden of proof, meaning that after suspending the transaction, the FIU will issue a prescription to the owner or person who possesses the property to come to the FIU and present the evidence regarding the source and ownership of the property. After receiving the requested documents and explanations, the FIU will undertake the analysis of the provided information to verify the owner and the source of the postponed assets.

On the basis of a precept, the FIU may restrict the disposal of property for up to 60 days for the purpose of ensuring its preservation if:

- During verification of the source of the property, in case there is a suspicion of money laundering, the owner or person who possesses the property fails to submit evidence certifying the legality of the source of the property to the FIU within 30 days as of the suspension of the transaction or of the imposition of restrictions on the use of the account; or
- There is suspicion that the property is used for terrorist financing.

If in case of suspicion of money laundering the legality of the source of the property is verified before the term expires, the FIU is required to immediately revoke the restrictions on the disposal of the property. If criminal proceedings have been commenced in the matter, a decision shall be taken on the revocation of the restrictions on the disposal of the property pursuant to the procedure provided by the laws regulating criminal procedure (seizing or freezing is possible with the permission of a judge).

In practice, the FIU will try to finalize its analysis at least two weeks before the expiry of the 90-day deadline. This two-week period is necessary for the prosecutor to make a decision regarding the commencement of the investigation and seizing or freezing the postponed assets. Depending on the case, the FIU may also contact the prosecutor much earlier, sometimes even before issuing the suspension of the transaction, for the purposes of more effective evidence collection (simultaneous surveillance activities, and so forth).

Moreover, according to the AML/CFT laws, the FIU may apply to an administrative court to restrict the disposal of property until identification of the actual owner for up to one year.

Notes

1. In one case, the compliance officer was able to request additional documents from the client and invite the client to come in the next day to obtain his funds. When the client arrived, he was arrested by the police.
2. An authorized disclosure is a disclosure that is made (a) before a person does the act prohibited by the AML/CFT Law; (b) while a person is doing the act prohibited

by the AML/CFT law, the act having begun at a point when the discloser did not know or suspect that the property is the proceeds of crime and the disclosure is made at the discloser's own initiative as soon as practicable after he or she first knew or suspected that the property is the proceeds of crime; or (c) after the act prohibited by the AML/CFT law, and is made at the discloser's own initiative as soon as practicable after the act.

3. Appropriate consent is the consent of an FIU officer to proceed with a prohibited act.

Sanitized Cases[1]

Economy A[2]

FIU Type: Administrative

Case 1

Money laundering and value-added tax (VAT) carousel fraud–carbon emission rights

Table C.1 Case 1

Offense	Money laundering
	Serious and organized fiscal fraud setting in motion complex mechanisms or using procedures with an international dimension (VAT carousel fraud–carbon emission rights)
Parties involved	Natural person
	Legal person
Sectors involved	Financial institutions
Channels used	International transfers
Economies involved	Germany, Romania, Switzerland
Disclosing entities	Bank
Warning signals	- The company's industry
	- The sector is susceptible to VAT fraud
	- The account was only used as a transit account

In 2010, the Belgian account of a company trading in energy products with a French manager was credited with various international transfers, mainly from Germany but also from Switzerland. Subsequently, transfers to Romania took place.

This company also held an account with a bank in Romania. Transactions for more than EUR 100 million took place on this account.

The Belgian Financial Intelligence Processing Unit (CTIF-CFI) was informed of these transactions through international cooperation.

In a few months' time the transactions in Belgium and Romania amounted to more than EUR 115 million.

In this file, CTIF-CFI used the provisions of the Law of 11 January 1993 enabling the FIU to halt a transaction for a period of two working days. CTIF-CFI postponed an amount of more than EUR 700,000.

According to the VAT support unit of the federal police, this company was known for VAT fraud related to carbon emission rights. The company purchased large carbon dioxide platforms (presumably abroad) and supplied "missing traders" in other member states.

The transactions in Germany indicated that the customers were probably located in Germany, where carbon emission trading is subject to the VAT.

Case 2

Other serious and organized fiscal fraud–involvement of untransparent financial centers

This case shows what role untransparent financial centers can play and how Belgian legislation enables CTIF-CFI to block money or assets for a period of two working days (see table C.2). International cooperation and cooperation among the various parties combating money laundering (administrative, police, and judicial) also play an important part in combating money laundering and recovering proceeds of illegal activities.

Table C.2 Case 2

Offense	Money laundering
	Serious and organized fiscal fraud setting in motion complex mechanisms or using procedures with an international dimension (other fraud)
Parties involved	Natural person
	Legal person
Sectors involved	Financial institutions
Channels used	International transfers
Jurisdictions involved	Belgium, Panama, Portugal, and Spain
Disclosing entities	Bank
Warning signals	- Succession of transfers (money transferred to Belgium is then transferred abroad that same day)
	- The transactions took place a few days after the account was opened
	- Belgium was used as a transit economy
	- Substantial amounts
	- Origin of the money (untransparent financial centers)

Four days after opening an account with a Belgian branch of a British bank, a Spanish national residing in Portugal without any link to Belgium received international transfers amounting to EUR 8,700,000 by order of a holding in Panama. He was the beneficial owner of this holding.

That same day he requested the bank to transfer EUR 8,500,000 to his account in Portugal to invest in real estate. The balance in the account was EUR 200,000.

The Belgian branch disclosed the suspicious transactions to CTIF-CFI and the parent company disclosed them to the British FIU.

CTIF-CFI's analysis showed the following:

- The Spanish national was suspected of carousel fraud and large-scale tax evasion in Spain.
- His Panamanian company already featured in an investigation in 2006 in the United Kingdom.

CTIF-CFI used its powers to freeze the remaining EUR 200,000 in the account with the Belgian branch and reported the file to the judicial authorities.

The British, Portuguese, and Spanish FIUs were immediately informed that the file had been reported and the amount of EUR 200,000 had been frozen.

CTIF-CFI informed the Central Office for Seizure and Confiscation and offered its assistance to facilitate the confiscation of EUR 200,000.

Shortly afterward, the customer wanted to transfer EUR 112,000,000 to an account with the same bank in Switzerland opened in the name of Panamanian and Cypriot holdings. He was the beneficial owner of these holdings as well. CTIF-CFI halted the transfer of EUR 112,000,000, which was also seized. This information was passed on to the British, Spanish, and Portuguese FIUs.

Economy B

FIU Type: Hybrid

A forged money transfer order was sent to a Bank in a European economy regarding the transfer of €3,000,000 from a company's account to an account maintained by an Economy B company with a bank in Economy B.

When the foreign company noticed the transfer, it communicated with the bank and, after they discovered that the money transfer order was forged, they notified the police. At the same time, the foreign bank contacted the bank in Economy B and informed them about what had happened, and requested that the funds be returned. The bank in Economy B immediately reported to Economy B's FIU all the facts, and filed an STR.

The next day, Economy B's FIU received an e-mail from the foreign FIU also informing them of all the facts, and then sent a request for assistance.

As a result of the above information, Economy B's FIU issued an administrative order forbidding the Economy B bank to allow the execution of any transactions regarding the €3,000,000 in the account. Following that, Economy B's FIU informed the foreign FIU about the administrative order and also that the suspect (owner of the Economy B company) had provided to the bank a sales contract, showing that the money was proceeds from the sale of several plots of land in Economy B.

In a few days, Economy B's FIU received a formal Rogatory Letter from the foreign authorities for freezing the €3,000,000 in the bank account, as well as all necessary documents required to issue a freeze order in Economy B. The documents included a signed declaration by the person referred to as the "purchaser" on the sales contract provided to Economy B bank by the suspect. This person is actually the owner of the foreign company that appeared to have been deceived. In his declaration he claimed never to have signed a sales contract with the suspect and furthermore that he was not even acquainted with him.

The owner of the bank account in Economy B, following an interview, gave his consent to return the relevant amount of money. Criminal charges were filed against this person but were eventually withdrawn because of lack of evidence on behalf of the foreign authorities.

The important issue was that with an administrative action on behalf of the FIU for the suspension of any transaction, it was possible to preserve the money at a critical point.

Economy C

FIU Type: Administrative

A bank in Economy C became aware of a foreign Securities Commission's investigation into Mr. A (a foreign national) over claims that he, along with Company A (a company domiciled in Economy C), convinced 22 individuals across the world to invest millions of dollars among them in a scheme falsely promising returns of up to 400 percent per week. Company A was beneficially owned by Mr. B (Economy C national). Mr. B was also an authorized signatory for banking purposes for one of Mr. A's companies in the United States, Company B. Mr. A was previously convicted of various fraudulent and money-laundering activities in the United States. Upon release from prison, Mr. A changed his name and appeared to be running fraudulent schemes once again. Company A was a client of the bank in Economy C.

In light of these factors, the bank in Economy C filed a suspicious activity report with Economy C's FIU, and also sought consent from that FIU under the Proceeds of Crime Act to continue dealing with Company A. The FIU withheld consent from the bank to conduct any transactions with Company A while it was making inquiries into the activities of the subjects.

While conducting enquiries into Company A and Mr. B, the FIU discovered that a foreign deposit of approximately US$1 million had been received into Company A's account from an overseas company looking to invest with Company A. Shortly after receipt of this deposit, Mr. B used some of the funds in Company A's account for personal expenses and then sought to transfer the remainder of these funds into Company B's account in the United States. The FIU immediately took steps to freeze all activity of Company A's account for 72 hours, in accordance with its governing statute, to enable it sufficient time to enquire into the suspicious transaction.

Enquiries revealed that Company A purported to be a licensed investment business in Economy C and that Mr. B was soliciting business overseas in conjunction with Company B and Mr. A. The subjects were using Company A as the vehicle for committing some of the fraudulent activity. Company A had never been licensed to conduct investment business in Economy C.

The FIU made relevant disclosures to local law enforcement and regulators, and to the relevant foreign FIU and the Securities Commission. Local law enforcement immediately took steps to secure a restraining order from the court over the accounts of Company A and Mr. B. Mr. B was arrested in Economy C and was ultimately convicted of operating an unlicensed investment company.

Mr. B was jailed for 15 months and orders of restitution were made to the benefit of the defrauded investors. The money that was frozen by the FIU and then subsequently restrained by order of the court was returned to investors. Mr. A, Mr. B, Company A, and Company B were also prosecuted by the Securities Commission and were found to have committed securities fraud by running a worldwide Ponzi scheme from which they profited. Mr. A and Mr. B (along with others) have each been fined US$335,000 and orders of restitution have been made totaling approximately US$4 million.

Economy D

FIU Type: Police

Between late 2009 and early 2010, victims in Foreign Economy A received cold calls from culprits purporting to be government officers of that jurisdiction. The culprits accused these victims of laundering the proceeds of crime and demanded that the victims transfer funds to designated accounts in Foreign Economy A and Economy D for temporary custody in order to prove their innocence, or else they would be arrested. Eventually, about US$1.2 million was remitted to three bank accounts in Economy D.

In late 2009, Economy D's FIU received confidential information about the suspicious remittances from Foreign Economy A. Immediate actions were taken by Economy D's FIU, which led to the identification of three bank accounts (Accounts 1, 2, and 3) that were opened by M and N, residents in Foreign Economy B. It also transpired that X withdrew funds from these accounts. Though the identity of X was unknown, Economy D's FIU immediately requested the banks to monitor the accounts and to alert the frontline staffs. At the same time, the financial intelligence was passed to Economy D's law enforcement authorities (LEAs) for investigation.

Afterward, a remittance of US$100,000 was made to Account 1 and a remittance of US$180,000 was made to Account 2. The FIU immediately refused to give consent to the banks to conduct further transactions. The LEA later identified the remitters, who were still unaware of the fraud.

In early 2010, a victim remitted US$180,000 to Account 3. The FIU refused to give consent to the bank to conduct further transactions and informed the LEA of the inward remittance. A few days later, X and Y went to the bank to withdraw the funds, and the bank immediately informed the FIU and LEA.

Officers of the LEA immediately rushed to the bank while the frontline staff delayed the withdrawal. As a result, X and Y were caught red-handed at the bank and the cash withdrawal seized. Bank documents and bank credit and debit cards of M, N, and Y were recovered from the residence of X. X was found to be a local resident and Y was found to be from Foreign Economy B.

As a result, X and Y were convicted of money laundering and sentenced to three and two years imprisonment, respectively. All the funds were returned to the victims.

Economy E

FIU Type: Administrative

While analyzing transactions carried out by natural person XX, Economy E's FIU noted that several obliged entities under the AML/CFT law reported the following data to the FIU within a short period of time (in less than a year):

- Cash deposits into XX's bank accounts held in a number of banks (a total of approximately €700,000)
- A money exchange transaction–purchase of effective foreign currency (a total of approximately €200,000)
- Cash deposits into bank accounts held by legal person Y, one of whose owners is XX. The stated purpose of the XX's fund transfers into Y's bank account was a *founder's loan to the legal person*. The total amount of cash transfers with this purpose was approximately €50,000.

XX owns 100 percent of the share of legal person Z, which is the owner of legal person Y, whose assets consist of nonmoney capital, including 250 hectares of land in the vicinity of a main road.

Following an analysis of all XX's bank accounts and the bank accounts held by Y and Z, the companies connected to X through the above-described ownership structure, the FIU suspected money laundering in this case and disseminated information to the competent authorities in Economy E (police and prosecutor's office). The prosecutor's office then requested an investigation of a number of persons suspected to have illegally sold 250 hectares of land owned by Z, which XX had acquired by purchasing company Y in the privatization process. It was suspected that the land was fraudulently grossly undervalued for privatization purposes and that there were abuses in the acquisition process and through fictitious land valuation. Police arrested a number of suspects, including XX.

The FIU received an STR from a bank reporting a noncash transfer from company Z's bank account to XX's bank account with the stated purpose of *loan repayment*. Since XX was under arrest, one of his bank account nominees, hereinafter referred to as AA, issued an order to the bank to transfer €700,000 to the account of XX's wife, hereinafter referred to as AB. AB then authorized a lawyer, hereinafter referred to as BB, to further transfer the funds from her account into the account of the privatization agency, thereby disbursing the first instalment of the purchase price of a company that was subject to privatization, in line with a *contract for sale of socially owned capital by public tender.* The privatized entity was legal person E, who owns dozens of hectares of land of the best quality. The bank reported the above transaction as suspicious, based on the following indicators for recognizing suspicious transactions and risk analysis applied:

- Transactions between private and business accounts with no clear economic purpose
- Transactions carried out through intermediaries and involving a large number of bank accounts
- Transactions carried out through several nominees.

Therefore, the FIU issued, based on the AML/CFT law, a written order to the bank to suspend the execution of the transaction on grounds of suspicion on money laundering. The FIU promptly informed the competent state authorities thereof, including the police and the prosecutor's office, so that they could undertake measures within their remit.

Client AB, through her lawyer BB (who is one of the nominees for the account), attempted to force the transfer of €700,000 to the privatization agency (as an instalment for purchasing the company) by exerting pressure on the bank officers. However, the investigative judge ordered seizure of the proceeds.

Epilogue: The procedure is still in progress, while the proceeds, that is, €700,000 together with a number of flats in Economy E and several hundreds of hectares of land, have been seized pending a final court decision.

This case is significant because it involved the entire AML/CFT system in Economy E, and each of its elements within its remit. The joint efforts resulted in indictments and seizure of money, flats, companies, and real estate held by XX.

Economy F

FIU Type: Administrative

The Economy F police received a criminal complaint from a government department involving fraud and theft. The facts related to the predicate offenses indicated that staff working in the government department colluded with an external crime syndicate to assist in obtaining copies of legitimate vendor payments, which were subsequently duplicated and processed to the benefit of various accounts indirectly linked to the syndicate. The initial loss exposure amounted to approximately US$573,000.

Police requested Economy F's FIU's assistance in blocking the accounts that received the proceeds of crime, with an additional request to identify other possible players.

The FIU interacted with the relevant accountable institutions and subsequently issued several postponement orders, resulting in US$317,000 of the initial proceeds being secured. This enabled the prosecuting authority to obtain a preservation order to secure the proceeds.

These interventions were brought immediately after the police provided proof of the nexus between the criminal offense and the funds that were still available in the identified bank accounts.

Upon analysis of the STRs and bank records received of the accounts, the FIU identified various other payments originating from different government departments, which were unknown to the police at that stage, amounting to US$9.5 million. A large portion of these funds were already dissipated. The FIU was also able to identify that beneficiary names of corporate entities were cloned, to create the impression that legitimate refunds were being paid by the government departments.

The FIU approached the various government departments, which were victim of the above-mentioned US$9.5 million fraud, to alert them accordingly. The FIU assisted in identifying the dates, amounts, and accounts that benefited from the additional fraud, which enabled the government departments to identify insiders within their ranks who were complicit in facilitating the fraud.

By sharing the information, the government departments and the FIU were able to:

• Engage banks and have fraudulent payments reversed and prevent fraudulent payments that were already loaded to the system awaiting processing (total losses recovered and prevented from dissipation amounted to US$3.5 million)
• Identify contractors that were complicit in assisting the syndicate with remote access to the network
• Have three employees arrested and convicted of fraud, corruption, and money laundering.

The police subsequently investigated a murder case and approached the FIU for assistance, because they had seized numerous checkbooks at a murder scene.

The FIU was able to link the details of the checkbooks to the beneficiary accounts of the US$9.5 million fraud case, mentioned above. On the face of it, the deceased had no link to the US$9.5 million fraud, but subsequent analysis and investigation revealed that the deceased co-opted individuals to open the accounts that received the proceeds of crime, whereafter he took complete control of the accounts and manipulated electronic fund transfer payment references to have beneficiaries disguised, including himself, under the name of a corporate entity. Subsequently, the majority of the funds were layered and "cross-fired" to various accounts, including those of attorneys' trust accounts.

The FIU confronted one of the lawyers with these facts, was shown proof, advised about the limitations associated with the legal-professional privilege, and requested a refund of these funds to a police "financial safe-keeping account."

The repayment of US$61,000 took place within a few days after the FIU requested the refund.

Other attorneys obtained proceeds via electronic fund transfers in lieu of property purchases. The relevant funds of these attorneys' trust accounts, in the amount of US$561,000, were placed under restraint, because they were unwilling to refund the money. These funds were not intervened because the law enforcement authority was able to obtain orders preventing the transfer of immovable properties.

The prosecuting authority also obtained restraining orders over immovable property amounting to US$1.6 million and other movable property valued at US$293,000. In total, more than US$6.1 million were preserved, or placed under restraint.

To date, four suspects have been convicted on charges of fraud, corruption, and money laundering. Sentences ranged from 10 years' imprisonment to suspended sentences. Some of the accused will be witnesses in the cases involving eight additional accused.

Economy G

FIU Type: Administrative

A bank in Economy G informed the FIU of a suspicious transaction on the account of a foreign natural person. The bank had been contacted by a foreign bank, which claimed that certain funds in this persons account originated from fraudulent activity, and the bank was therefore requesting that the bank in Economy G return said funds. A few days later, the FIU received new STRs with similar contents from the bank. The analysis of the data and documentation showed that most probably the cases were connected, since all persons had residence in a small town in a neighboring economy.

The FIU started with the extensive collection of data and documentation on similar cases from all banks in Economy G and discovered that 8 foreign citizens had 12 transaction accounts in 2 banks. At the same time, at least four other persons with the same place of residence tried to open the transaction accounts in the bank. The accounts were opened for just one month, and the analysis of transactions on all accounts for this period showed that the transactions to the credit of the accounts were exclusively transfers of foreign natural persons from the United Kingdom and the United States. Between three and seven transfers arrived to each account, but the transactions to the debt of the account were just cash withdrawals. Total turnover to the credit of all 12 accounts was US$310,000 and GB£80,000, and all transactions referred to the "purchase of the vehicle" via the World Wide Web. The FIU informed the police and state prosecutor's office of its findings, stating as the reasons for suspicion that all eight persons had committed the criminal offense of money laundering by cash withdrawals, with which they tried to hide the person, actually disposing of the funds originating from the criminal offense of fraud.

The FIU ordered the postponement of two transactions of two accounts, namely cash withdrawals in the amounts of GB£7,500 and €7,500, informed the police and state prosecutor's office, and proposed the provisional securing of the illegally derived assets. The FIU also initiated the temporary seizure of all remaining funds at those two accounts. Based on the state prosecutor office's proposal, the court temporarily seized US$60,000 and GB£7,500 at four trans-action accounts for the period of three months, which was then prolonged twice each time for three months. The complete criminal file was later transferred to the neighboring economy, from which the suspects arrived.

During the postponement period the FIU was in contact with the police. Even before that, the bank had to simultaneously report to the FIU every transaction in the account. When the cash withdrawal was announced, the FIU informed the police and instructed the bank to hold the client (when he attempted to perform the cash withdrawal) in the bank as long as possible. In this way, the FIU blocked both amounts and the police arrested both perpetrators.

Economy H

FIU Type: Administrative

A bank reported to Economy H's FIU that one of its clients, a foreign citizen, owned a term-deposit savings account, and certain funds in that account were fixed-term deposited for one year. This client (Economy X national) requested that the bank annul the deposit earlier than the one-year term and pay him all the funds he had at the bank.

However, the bank's AML compliance officer, using publicly available data sources, discovered that criminal proceedings had been instituted against the client in the client's domicile economy on the suspicion of the criminal act of abuse of office and money laundering. On the basis of this information, the bank's AML compliance officer designated the transactions as supicious.

After receiving the STR, the FIU searched its database, collected data, ana-lyzed the data, and checked the data from available sources. Within the FIU's database, several cash transactions executed by the suspected client had already been recorded. These transactions were related to deposits, depositing cash and withdrawing funds from the savings account.

At the same time, the FIU communicated with the FIU of Economy X, and after intensive correspondence, Economy H's FIU received a confirmation that criminal proceedings had been instituted against this person, as indicated by the bank.

Moreover, this foreign FIU requested the FIU to pospone the execution of the transactions from the account of the suspected client. The foreign FIU also requested the FIU to check whether the same client had opened accounts with other banks, and if so, to temporarily postpone the funds in those accounts.

In the meantime, Economy H's FIU found out that this person owned an account with another bank in Economy H. Thus, in accordance with the AML/CFT law, the FIU ordered both banks to postpone the execution of all transactions on these accounts, that is, the withdrawal of funds in the amount of €68,600 from the accounts, for 72 hours.

At the same time, the foreign FIU and the local prosecutor's office and police were notified of the postpoment of the transactions. Later, funds in the amount of €68,600 were frozen by Economy H's court on a basis of a Rogatory Letter received from Economy's X judicial authorities.

Economy I

FIU Type: Administrative

The FIU of Economy I was informed about activity of an international organized group. The group organized hacker attacks in the United States and attempted to launder proceeds in Economy I. Two foreign citizens opened accounts in Economy I and received small (US$50 to US$100) transfers from foreign jurisdictions. Then they started to receive much larger transfers (up to US$500,000). Upon request of the bank, the clients provided explanations and produced documents. That only escalated the suspicions and led to reporting to the FIU. Meanwhile, the banks of the victims informed the Economy I banks of the hacked accounts.

The FIU only had information from the banks (including the message from the banks of the victims). One bank in Economy I postponed the transaction for two days (the maximum period for postponement imposed by the bank according to the AML/CTF law).

The FIU issued its own postponement order for one account (for the maximum allowed five-day period) and extended the postponement imposed by another bank for five more days. In total, transactions of US$1.4 million were postponed.

The FIU requested information from:

- Foreign FIU 1, which was the economy of the victims
- Foreign FIU 2, which was the economy of persons who opened the account.

Foreign FIU 2 provided extensive information on the activity of the organized group and informed the requesting FIU that it started a joint investigation with the law enforcement agencies. In addition, foreign FIU 2 requested the FIU of Economy I to postpone transactions for 30 days.

The FIU of Economy I issued the new postponement orders on behalf of foreign FIU 2 for 30 days (such postponement is not limited in time by the AML/CTF law of Economy I).

The FIU received complaints from the legitimate owners of the money via the foreign law enforcement agency. The FIU sent a case to its own law enforcement authority, which started surveillance of two suspects and established contacts with the bank officers.

Police in Economy I opened a criminal case, arrested the suspects, and applied to the court for a freeze order (until the final sentence). The court granted the request and the money was frozen until the criminal procedure was concluded.

Notes

1. Sanitized cases presented in this paper were provided by the following FIUs: Belgium; Bermuda; Cyprus; Estonia; Hong Kong SAR, China; Montenegro; Serbia; Slovenia; South Africa; and Ukraine. The cases that FIUs chose to provide sought to highlight "successful" cases involving FIU use of the postponement power. This collection of cases does not reflect the full ambit of FIU experiences and challenges when exercising this power.
2. Sanitized Cases previously published by Belgium in the CTIF-CFI's "17th Annual Report 2010," pp. 49–51.

Template

As can be seen from the sample template that appears below, a postponement order is a more complex document than might at first be expected. There are many aspects and issues that need to be addressed to ensure that an order is valid and, to the extent possible, unassailable. Moreover, it is a document that serves not only to communicate instructions to the reporting entity to which it is addressed, but it also provides information and direction to other state bodies that may be recipients of copies of the order.

One of the hallmarks of the exercise of administrative and judicial powers in any society is that authority be exercised fairly and consistently, and not in an arbitrary or ad-hoc manner. In this regard, given the multiplicity of factors that come into play in a decision to order the postponement of a suspicious transaction, a template serves two very important purposes:

- It is a guide to the user (the FIU) on all of the issues that need to be addressed in an order.
- By its design and function, it helps assure consistency of practice, and also serves to streamline and speed up the process of preparation of the order.

FIUs are well advised to make use of a template for the purpose of preparing postponement orders. They may use one like the one below, or modify it, or develop a variant that conforms to established practice in their own jurisdiction. In deciding on a format or template, however, FIUs are advised to take note of the issues addressed in this template.

Postponement Order/Notice

[Delete whichever is not applicable]

[Date]

Compliance Officer

[Name of reporting institution]

[Address]

Re: Order/Notice to Postpone a Suspicious Transaction

Dear Sir/Madam:

The .... [Insert name of FIU] is conducting a money-laundering/ terrorist-financing enquiry into matters concerning the following subject(s)[1]:

Name of Subject:

Date of Birth (if applicable):

Address:

On a basis of paragraph ... [Insert number of paragraph] of article ... [Insert number of article] of the law .... [Insert title of the law] we are issuing the following

Order/Notice

1. Transaction/all transactions .... [Type of suspended transaction] against .... [Insert Subject or Account Owner, if applicable] account [If applicable] .... [Account type and number, if applicable] in the amount of .... [Value of transaction], in relation to which on .... [Insert the date] an order/notice has been given by .... [Insert the name of person, who gave the order to the reporting entity] to .... [Describe the attempted transaction and the name and address of recipient/beneficiary of transaction], should be postponed.

2. The above-mentioned transaction should be postponed for a period of .... [Insert time] hours commencing at .... [Insert time and date] or until an earlier repeal of this order.

Explanation[2]

According to ... [Insert number of paragraph] of ... [Insert number of article] of the law .... [Insert the title of the law] the .... [Insert name of FIU] is authorized to postpone a suspicious transaction under the following conditions: .... [Insert the triggers/conditions expressly provided in the law].

The postponement of a transaction can last a maximum of .... [Insert the maximum duration] hours and [Option 1] cannot be extended; [Option 2] can be extended for .... [Insert number of extensions and maximum duration of the extended postponement].

[Option 1] There is no right to appeal this order/notice.

[Option 2] According to .... [Insert number of paragraph] of ... [Insert number of article] of the law .... [Insert the title of the law] a right of appeal this order may be exercised by ...... [Insert the name of the legal/natural person that has the statutory right to appeal the postponement order] and must be filed within .... [Insert time period as prescribed in the legislation].

Please note that the law .... [Insert details of the law/statutory authority] establishes a criminal/administrative offense for any institution that fails, without reasonable excuse, to comply with this Order. The law ……. **[Insert the law/statutory authority]** also prohibits disclosure of the fact that this transaction has been postponed to the client/subject of transaction or to any other unauthorized person.

We would appreciate your written acknowledgment of receipt of this Order/Notice.

Yours Faithfully,

[Insert name]

Director of the **[name of FIU]**

Notes

1. Subjects can be natural and/or legal persons.
2. Depending on their domestic statutory requirements, jurisdictions may add in the explanatory part additional factual or legal information related to the case in question.

Survey Participants

The following economies participated in the World Bank–Egmont Group survey. The FIUs of the bolded economies have the power to postpone a suspicious transaction.

1. **Albania**
2. Andorra
3. Argentina[1]
4. **Armenia**
5. Aruba
6. **Austria**
7. **Azerbaijan**
8. **The Bahamas**
9. Bahrain
10. **Belarus**
11. **Belgium**
12. **Bermuda**
13. **Bolivia**
14. **Bosnia and Herzegovina**
15. **British Virgin Islands**
16. **Bulgaria**
17. Canada
18. Chile
19. **Costa Rica**
20. **Croatia**
21. Curacao
22. **Cyprus**
23. **Czech Republic**
24. **Denmark**
25. Estonia
26. Fiji
27. **Finland**
28. France

29. FYR of Macedonia
30. **Gibraltar**
31. **Greece**
32. Grenada
33. **Guernsey**
34. Honduras
35. **Hong Kong SAR, China**
36. **Hungary**
37. India
38. **Indonesia**
39. **Ireland**
40. Isle of Man
41. **Italy**
42. **Jamaica**
43. Japan
44. **Jersey**
45. **Kazakhstan**
46. **Latvia**
47. **Lebanon**
48. **Lithuania**
49. **Luxemburg**
50. Macao SAR, China
51. Malaysia
52. **Mali**
53. **Malta**
54. Mexico
55. **Moldova**
56. **Monaco**
57. **Montenegro**
58. **Morocco**
59. **Namibia**
60. **Nigeria**
61. **Norway**
62. Paraguay
63. Peru
64. Philippines
65. **Poland**
66. Portugal
67. Qatar
68. **Romania**
69. **Russian Federation**
70. **San Marino**
71. **Senegal**
72. **Serbia**

73. **Seychelles**
74. **Slovak Republic**
75. **Slovenia**
76. **South Africa**
77. Spain
78. Sweden
79. Taiwan, China
80. **Tajikistan**
81. **Thailand**
82. **Trinidad & Tobago**
83. **Tunisia**
84. Turkey
85. **Turkmenistan**
86. Turks & Caicos Islands
87. **Ukraine**
88. United States

Note

1. Following its participation in this survey, the AML/CFT law in Argentina was amended in 2012 giving its FIU the power to postpone suspicious transactions.

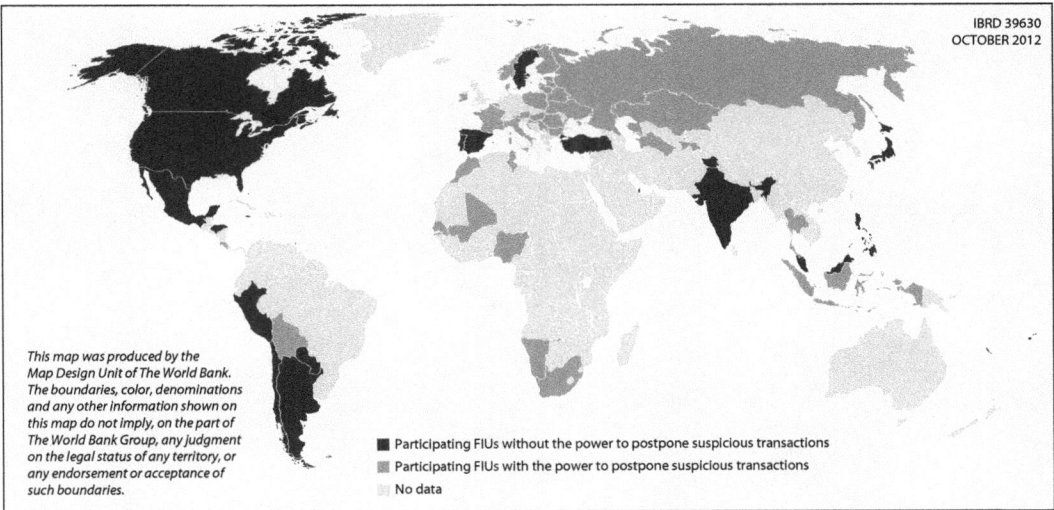

REFERENCES

CTIF-CFI (Belgian Financial Intelligence Processing Unit). 2010. "17th Annual Report." Brussels, Belgium.

IMF (International Monetary Fund) and World Bank. 2004. *Financial Intelligence Units— An Overview*. Washington, DC: International Monetary Fund and World Bank.

Stephenson, Kevin, Jean-Pierre Brun, Larissa Gray, and Clive Scott. 2011. *Barriers to Assets Recovery*. Washington, DC: World Bank–United Nations Office on Drugs and Crime.

UNODC (United Nations Office on Drugs and Crime). 2010. *The Globalization of Crime—A Transnational Organized Crime Threat Assessment*. Vienna: UNODC.

Websites

- Egmont Group: http://www.egmontgroup.org.
- Egmont Group "Annual Report 2010–2011": http://www.egmontgroup.org/news-and-events/news/2011/12/23/2010-2011-egmont-group-annual-report.
- European Commission Proposal for a Directive of the European Parliament and of the Council on the Freezing and Confiscation of Proceeds of Crime in the European Union, COM (2012) 85 final, Brussels, 12.3.2012: http://eur-lex.europa.eu/LexUriServ/LexUriServ.do?uri=COM:2012:0085:FIN:EN:PDF.
- Financial Action Task Force (FATF): http://www.fatf-gafi.org/pages/aboutus/.
- Financial Action Task Force (FATF) Recommendations: http://www.fatf-gafi.org/topics/fatfrecommendations/documents/fatfrecommendations2012.html.
- Palermo Convention (United Nations Convention against Transnational Organized Crime, UNTOC): http://www.unodc.org/unodc/en/treaties/CTOC/index.html.
- Strasbourg Convention (1990 Council of Europe Convention on Laundering, Search, Seizure and Confiscation of the Proceeds from Crime): http://conventions.coe.int.
- United Nations Convention against Corruption (UNCAC): http://www.unodc.org/unodc/en/treaties/CAC/index.html.
- UNSC (United Nations Security Council) Resolution 1267 (1999): http://www.un.org/Docs/sc/committees/1267/1267ResEng.htm.
- UNSC (United Nations Security Council) Resolution 1373 (2001): http://www.un.org/Docs/scres/2001/sc2001.htm.
- UNSC (United Nations Security Council) Resolution 1735 (2006): http://www.un.org/Docs/sc/unsc_resolutions06.htm.

Warsaw Convention (Council of Europe Convention on Laundering, Search, Seizure and Confiscation of the Proceeds from Crime and on the Financing of Terrorism: http://conventions.coe.int.

www.ingramcontent.com/pod-product-compliance
Lightning Source LLC
Chambersburg PA
CBHW080618270326
41928CB00016B/3111